Fear of a Black P***s

Fear of a Black P***s

✦

Race, Class and the 21st Century Slave

Gordon Manning

iUniverse, Inc.
New York Lincoln Shanghai

Fear of a Black P***s
Race, Class and the 21st Century Slave

iUniverse books may be ordered through booksellers or by contacting:

iUniverse
2021 Pine Lake Road, Suite 100
Lincoln, NE 68512
www.iuniverse.com
1-800-Authors (1-800-288-4677)

ISBN: 978-0-595-44857-9 (pbk)
ISBN: 978-0-595-89180-1 (ebk)

Printed in the United States of America

For
The
Brothers and Sisters
Who've
Had Enough

Contents

"Life has frightened me now and then, and if I've ever shown uncommon bravery, I've failed to notice it. I still dream big at times, but when my dreams pull apart, as they sometimes do, I don't press the panic button. Only a chosen few are selected to rise above their true height ..."

—**Gordon Parks**

INTRODUCTION

I had a tough time coming up with the introduction to this book. It felt like every time I tried to express my true intentions for writing it I found myself searching for the right words that fit. So of course I began to second guess myself, wondering if I was on the right track or simply just trying to make a "statement." "What are you *really* trying to say?" became my favorite question of the day as I endured the countless revisions, creative roadblocks and late night bouts with insomnia that I (and every other writer I know) inevitably faces while trying to complete a project. I thought back to the times I ran down the idea for *Fear of a Black Penis* to a couple close relatives in the hopes that they would "co-sign" the concept. Usually the exchange went something like this; I'd be like; "So whatchu think huh?" And they'd be like; (brief pause) "Sounds interesting but you know you need to change that title right?" Then I'm like; "Uhm, well ..." Then they'd come back with; "I'm just sayin,' are you sure you want to name it *that*? "Just think about it that's all, I mean how am I supposed to read a book with that kind of title on the bus?? ..." Right then and there I realized I might just be on to something. On top of that I remembered what a good friend of mine had told me one day in casual conversation. "Look here man, it's like this; sometimes you just gotta put your "nuts" on the table bruh ... simple as that." At that point I stopped focusing on the reaction it might provoke in others and began concentrating on what *I* was truly trying to say. This was the turning point. Along the way I learned many valuable lessons. First of which was the importance of honoring that unique voice only you possess but are often afraid of letting the world hear. Secondly, I realized the value of trusting your own instincts. In other words my friends this book is about me as much as it is about you. Better yet it is about *us,* and the way we see ourselves and each other. But perhaps most importantly it is about where we are headed. You see my friends the *Fear of a Black Penis* is really just a misrepresentation of the ultimate creative force in existence today. Or rather, the fear of a Black GENIUS. It's like this; some people love animals. Some people eat animals. Most people *say* they love animals and eat them anyway! In a nutshell, this is America folks. Home of the brave. Land of the free. Land of opportunity. Home of opportunists. And the rest of us? Well, we just hang on for dear life till the train comes to a complete stop. So far away from home, so close to what might have been. I know one thing though, it's hard as hell to let go. To trade in all of the illusions, cravings and attachments of today for the hope of a brighter, more prosperous tomorrow. But what else is there? I mean, at the end of the day when it's all said and done all we have is US right? Ain't that right brothers and sisters? Well ain't it?

G.

1

"WHERE Y'ALL AT?"

So now all of a sudden everybody's got an opinion. Talk radio lines across the country are crammed, jammed and slammed with rabid callers practically foaming at the mouth to add their two cents to the conversation. It's easy to see why. Seems like every other week another public figure, comedian, politician or disc jockey is sticking his (her) foot in their mouth. It's as if they just can't help themselves. Then comes the usual "insensitive," "despicable" and just "flat out racist" outcry that follows. Two minutes after that we're goin' ballistic, calling them every "pig," "MF," "sleazebag" and "low life" under the sun. And then we're demanding their job, head and everything else on a platter, picketing in front of their corporate headquarters with home-made cardboard signs, rusty bullhorns and determined frowns. All this is followed by the standard apology; "I said a bad thing, but I'm a good person ..." We know you are. Nevertheless, the power of words is somethin' serious people. Strangely enough though these days it's the cruelty of the words we use towards each other that is sabotaging our own (r)evolution. And that's real. So let's talk about the power of YOU for a moment. Or the lack thereof. It doesn't take a rocket scientist to see that the times really are-a-changin.' Especially for those of us in the "colored section." You can feel it in the air. You can see it on the street. Things are moving *fast* folks, faster than ever before. Within the past few months we've all felt the heat go up a notch or three as we adjust to the latest headline/scandal. You simply can't say the same things you could've just five, ten years ago. Whether it's the N-word, B-word, F-word or any other word deemed offensive or racist you better make sure you get a grip on them lips before you find yourself in the hot seat. But who is really getting burned at the end of the day? And would you have been as offended by those hateful remarks if your "brother" had said them? Does it even matter? In this country you can slip, fall, get back up, dust yourself off and wind up richer than ever before! That's if you've got the "juice." Or your story's titillating enough to attract viewers/voyeurs. It's not even about freedom of speech anymore. It's the *exposure* that matters. So even though we've all said (or at least thought) the same damn thing at one point or another in our lives these days you're better off keeping it to yourself. That is if you want to keep your day job. But what does that say about the times we live in? More importantly, what in the *hell* is on your mind these days brothers and sisters? Huh? That's all I want to know. Let me tell you what's on mine. Lately I've been talking to myself more than usual. Asking ME some real serious questions like; "Self, just who is allowed to call your beautiful Black sister a "nappy headed ho," jiggaboo, chicken head or freak toy?" Do I, as a Black man get a pass even though I've been known to "make it rain on them hoes" once or thrice in my checkered past? What's that all about? You'll soon see my friends, you'll soon see … But if you're hip enough to peep the writing on the wall you already know precisely who's gonna be targeted next. Just don't say I didn't warn you.

See, these days you have to give your mind the same advice you'd give a child, spouse or best friend. Things like; "Just take your time baby, it's gon' be alright." Or "Don't let 'em get to you honey just B-R-E-A-T-H-E." But even after you exhale sometimes you still end up wondering what planet you're really living on. Who knew? Guess your outlook all depends on what side of the fence you sit on. Or simply put, your state of mind. 'Cause at the end of the day how you deal with any situation comes down to just that, your state of mind. And it's cool if you can handle it. 'Cause that's really all you've got to hold on to once the s**t hits the fan. All the drama, "changes," love, pain, good times, tears and yes my friends, the fear of a Black penis …

YOU CAN'T BE SERIOUS?

Sure I am. We live in a society where everything is cheap/chic, processed, disposable … Last week they recalled cat food. Week before that it was baby food, then peanut butter, and so on and so forth. Seven year olds are now getting cell phones for Christmas. In a few years even they'll be extinct. Nine year olds are bringing baggies of crack to school for "Show and Tell!" You don't hear me though. You just say; "Damn, what is this world comin' to?" It's hard to watch the evening news anymore. Why? Because we're creating a generation of young people afraid to answer their true calling that's why. And deep down inside we know it. Yet we still look the other way. Yes my friends, things are moving at lightning speed. But there's still a snack machine in every corner for you to get your fix. Whether it's energy drinks, granola bars, ham and cheese sandwiches or beef jerky it's all there for you. And a portable ATM machine right beside it. Always some boost or blast to help us make it through the day and the roller coaster we call the "real world." But why do we even need so much energy in the first place? WHAT'S THE RUSH? Why are we moving so fast and keeping ourselves so doggone distracted that what's *really* important is the last option on our "to do list?" Some of you are so much in a hurry you don't even have time to put on your seat belt! We've got high definition television, satellite radio, and more access to information than ever before. And we still want more. I must admit we've come a long way since the sit-ins, boycotts, riots, marches, picket lines and picket signs of the sixties. But then again measuring our evolution (as a people) by these standards may not be the most accurate barometer of where we currently stand. You'll probably get a clearer picture of what's really goin' on by simply looking into a child or teenager's eyes. See, there are many conflicting emotions swirling around on the inside of Black people these days as we so eagerly proclaim "Aw, life is good man!" to anyone who asks.

And life very well may be good for those of you who've embraced and become fully integrated into "the system." But for those of us who have resisted the urge to completely merge, the road can be a bit rockier. For me, sometimes it's easier to just reminisce about how things used to be rather than look ahead to a future that looks hazier than I once pictured it. I know I'm not alone. It's just that we have different ways of dealing with the pressure. Truth is, most of us are simply too caught up in our daily routines to STOP for even five minutes. If its not getting the kids ready for school its cleaning the garage, if its not mowing the lawn its hosting the dinner party, watching the ball game, punching the clock etc ... leaving us little to no time for true reflection much less ... well, *anything* else. I know. It is what it is. But I can't help but remember how it used to be.

THEN

When I was coming up you couldn't walk into a Black living/family room without seeing a *JET* or *Ebony* magazine spread out on the coffee table. This was as natural as seeing your brotha or sista sportin' a "fro" or "natural" on their heads. It was simply a sign of the times. These magazines often sparked conversation about current events as well as issues of the day that affected Black people. They were also used occasionally as coasters for whatever your particular beverage of choice happened to be. You'd flip through the pages, check the announcements, cover story and photographs before making your way to the back to peep the "Beauty of the Week." At least that's what I did. A lot of you out there know what I'm talkin' about. A few of you still subscribe to one or more of these magazines to this day. They were very instrumental in how we looked at ourselves at a time when our presence in the media, airwaves and sound scapes of mainstream American society was less commonplace than it is today. There was always a certain excitement in wondering which Black entertainer, famous athlete or politician would be gracing the latest issue. Matter of fact just being on the cover of *JET* or *Ebony* seemed like such an accomplishment back then, maybe because it was so rare that we got to see one another as a normal well-adjusted and prosperous people considering the "dark" history of our existence in this country up to that point. But things have definitely changed since the good ole days of the 1970's/early 80's. I do know a couple folks who've saved every last issue of *Ebony* and *JET* from then till now. They keep them in the attic or garage in old dusty crates and boxes probably thinking they'll be worth something one day. Fortunately I'm old enough to remember some of the good ol' days and still look upon them with fond memories and a smile on my face.

NOW

You can't even raise your voice at the airport. And the way things look pretty soon you'll have to strip down to your damn drawers just to get through the security check and onto the plane. Forget the "magic wand." In a couple years it'll be "Ah yes sir, everything but your drawers …" "Strictly for your own safety (wink wink)." Man, I still remember the days when you could smoke *on* the plane! But of course that was then. And this is now. A lot has changed in America over the past fifteen, twenty years or so. White people are screaming. Black people are dreaming. And we've all reached a serious fork in the road. First it was the Worldwide Web (Cyber Age) which literally opened the flood gates to this endless ocean of information we now have access to. Chat lines, blogs, e-mails and text messages have replaced books and genuine human interaction. And the technology! The technology is moving so fast that if you're not hip to the new lingo it's easy to get left behind. Our children are growing up smarter, yet "dumber" than at any other point in history. They are choosing the streets, "freaks," and lowered expectations of whatever's HOT to the wisdom of their elders and guardian angels. In other words, something's missing. What is it? Could it be that after all the blood, sweat, years, and tears of our existence in this country we have somehow lost our way as a people? Certainly looks like it. I know this much. Somewhere along the way we lost confidence in EACH OTHER. And so, here we are at the dawn of a new millennium with as many unresolved issues and unanswered questions as any other time in our colorful history. So how 'bout we get to it and see if we can come to some type of understanding as to who, what, where, when and HOW we are. Sound like a good idea brothers and sisters? Okay then. Cool.

They say we only use ten percent of our brains, if that. Sounds about right. There are geniuses everywhere you look in the Black community. Mathematicians, computer wizards, CEO's, "Mothers of the Year." And still we've got million dollar minds selling bootleg CDs and DVDs on practically every corner of the 'hood, dope boys lurking in the shadows and slicksters tryin' to con you out of everything but your socks. First thing you should know though is that you've been here before. With a different name no doubt, minus the designer shades, shoes and SUV of course, but here nonetheless. And in all your past lives you have embodied the darkness as well as the light. The whole thing baby. You have to remember life hasn't always just been get married, have kids, buy your first house and spend the next thirty, forty years paying it off despite today's social norms and the dream you've been sold. Oh no brothers and sisters. From the beginning of time you have had much more to offer humanity than jumping high and "rocking the mic." BELIEVE THAT! Which means you have a unique responsibility to the world given the extraordinary amount of gifts you have been blessed with. The question is; are you prepared to finally share these gifts with the world or continue to keep them stored away in the attic only to collect more dust and cobwebs? It's up to you. After all, only you know how it feels to be Black correct? But feelings are mighty hard to describe these days, especially given the numerous challenges we now face collectively as a people. All this to say that now is the perfect time to dig deeper into what's really goin' down on your block, 'round your corner, in yo' 'hood, and in your HEAD. In order to do this though you must first ask yourself a very serious question:

"What does it really mean to be FREE?"

Take your time now. For this question requires quite a bit more soul-searching than; "Baby, you think my butt look big in these jeans?" Seriously folks, we've been here too long to go out like that. We've heard for many years now that the "mind is a terrible thing to waste." But the new slogan seems to be "As long as I got "mines" I'm good ..." Meanwhile, our brains continue to have *minds* of their own, running wild and loose in any and every direction. That is, every direction but UP. It's almost as if we still believe we belong on the back of the bus. Think I'm crazy? All you gotta do is take a ride on your local public transportation system one day to see for yourself. Then get back to me sister. But like I was saying, this constant relentless search for freedom as well as the "WHO I" has caused many of us to re-examine, and in some cases redefine our "Blackness" in the current scheme of things. Unfortunately the mirror has a tendency to lie sometimes, causing us to see whatever it is we choose to and not what's right in front of our face. It's like when you see a photograph of yourself and blurt out; "I *do not* look like that!" Of course you do honey. Can't you see? But what is it you see when you look into my eyes? Do you see pride, fear, the pimple on my face or the brilliance on my mind? Perhaps you see yourself. I know what I see when I look in yours. And it's probably not what you think.

In any event, just last year big lips were still "soup coolers" where I'm from. I'm only kidding, but you'd think they were more precious than rubies the way these "supermodels" have suddenly made them all the rage in popular culture. They call it the "European look." Imagine that? But the real question is where does that leave Condoleezza Rice? Just because we happen to share the same shade does that automatically make her my sista? Is there even a manual for WHAT BLACK IS? Perhaps it's just a state of mind like everything else. Or maybe that particular energy field shared by the millions of people who can actually bask in the sun without having to drown in SPF#30. For many of you Black means voting Democratic in the upcoming presidential race (though not necessarily for the "colored" candidate). And every-body knows that Black on a military base in Germany is quite differ-ent than Black on the "block" or in the ghetto. Or is it? And not all of us live in the ghetto for that matter. So lately I've been asking myself what this Black thang is really all about. And I've come to the conclu-sion it's more like a life preserver to stay afloat from all the bull***t goin' on in and around us. It's how we're able to roll with the punches, go with the flow, take a lickin,' keep on tickin' and all the rest, hoping that one day, *someday* it'll all make sense.

In the meantime, whiter teeth won't necessarily improve your self-image, though them white strips may make you feel like "cheesing" a bit more for the camera than before. As far as dropping that twenty-five, forty pounds or so you still may not like what you see in the mir-ror! It's all about perception. Truth is you can make yourself believe anything you want to for whatever reason you need to. Case in point, for years I led myself to believe that we're all in this together. But recently my mind has been telling me to watch my damn back! From a very young age I was taught how the world is (cold) and what I need to do to make it through the blizzard, even if that means donning dif-ferent sweaters, coats, hats and gloves in order to stay warm. I learned to despise Mondays and welcome Fridays, to let loose on Saturdays and dry out on Sundays. Just in time to iron my slacks and head right back into the rat race. Why is this so? It's like this. Our memories are both wonderful and painful. So we learn to filter the pleasant and seek protection from the uncomfortable. And Black folks for better or worse, richer or poorer are taught to keep it moving. 'Cause in this country we all know that's the only way to get ahead. Meanwhile our brains are constantly being rinsed, washed, and hung out to dry to such an extent that when things start to get too much to handle we make a conscious effort to "zone out." Plug in our headphones, ear-pieces and pump up the volume. Yet underneath all of this each of us still believes we are special deep down inside. The problem is we've been taught to base our self-worth on such ridiculous illusions as appearance, occupation, and financial status. And so we start seeing the world, our position in it, and most importantly EACH OTHER in terms of these illusions. So why exactly do our minds go haywire at certain times, driving us to eat, drink, smoke, and engage in all types of bizarre behavior just to numb the pain and dilute our own not so pleasant memories? I wish I knew. Here's what I do know though. All of us come into this world with at least five senses. But as the reality of life's ups and downs sets in little by little we lose our minds (Blacks especially). It's because Blackness is contagious. And if you're not careful and begin to believe what they say when it comes to the grade of your particular shade, you might just lose your damn mind too!

BLACK: (1) very dark in color <his face was *black* with rage> (2a) having dark skin, hair, and eyes: SWARTHY (3) HEAVY, SERIOUS (4) DIRTY, SOILED <hands *black* with grime> (5b) reflecting or transmitting little or no light (6a) thoroughly sinister or evil: WICKED (b) indicative of condemnation or discredit <got a black mark for being late> (7) connected with or invoking the supernatural and especially the devil <*black* magic> (8a) very sad, gloomy, or calamitous (b) marked by the occurrence of disaster <*black* Friday> 9) characterized by hostility or angry discontent: SULLEN <*black* resentment filled his heart> … (**Merriam Webster**)

Sound like YOU? … Rumor has it we became "Black" sometime around the late 60's or so. That's what I've been told anyway. In fact, many of you are still young enough to remember when "Black *was* Beautiful." In the 70's when I was a child you didn't have to look very far to see what this "Blackness" thing was all about. All you had to do was listen to Marvin's *What's Goin On,* Miles' *Bitches' Brew* or Bob's *Exodus* to see what time it was. Oh, and pretty much *anything* from the Godfather of Soul. If music wasn't your bag then you could just pull the Afro pick from out your back pocket, grab the dashiki out the closet or head on into the living room and flip through that *Jet* magazine to get your mind right. And can't forget the love and togetherness you felt at the cookout or house party. Good times … and all in the spirit of unity, family, and fun. This is what I remember. And so my image of "Blackness" looks a bit different than Mr. Webster's. May I?

BLACK: (1) STRENGTH, CREATIVITY extreme intelligence: ORIGINALITY < GRACE, ELEGANCE <that boy can blow that horn, sure he ain't got no *black* in him? INNOVATIVE (2) supremely gifted, uniquely talented, REGAL scarred yet RESILIENT … <Say it loud!> (b) a once proud, dignified race <THEY BUILT THE PYRAMIDS> (c) able to create new forms and ways of seeing things <i.e. rock n roll, jazz, blues, hip-hop, etc.> (3) COMPAS-SIONATE (d) highly spiritual (4) DOMINANT < i.e. the *black*er the berry, sweeter the juice> (e) no sugar, no cream (5) EXQUISITE …

Ah yes! That's more like it. And in that case, some of my best friends really *are* … Anyway, naturally all of us owe our color (or lack thereof) to the amount of melanin (pigment) or chlorine in our gene pool. Walk through any Black neighborhood and you'll see about a million different shades of Black from "high yella" to "blurple." And if you're anything like me you probably know at least five cats named "Black," "Reds," or "Yella" right in your own neighborhood. But with all of this diversity out there in the Black community … Hold up a second; can we even say there is such a thing as a Black "community" anymore? I know there used to be one. The word itself, comm-UNITY implies some sort of collective voice or group vision, some-thing that seems to be sadly missing these days. Most of us are too invested in our own individual everyday struggle to for this concept to even cross our minds. When I say vision I mean more than just a par-ticular movement or leader per se, more like a direction or aim. That is, aside from gettin' PAID … Think about it, I mean, it's easy to visualize all Black people doing the Electric Slide at the wedding reception, or stepping up for another plate of ribs and spiked punch at the barbecue. But when it comes to any sort of unified strength, agenda or power we seem to always come up short. The sad thing is, this lack of togetherness is not limited to the Black man/woman of North America, but to most places where there is a large concentration of African people. It's true. And because of this lack of organization we now seem to be running in place, doin' the "Hammer Dance" or imitating the same behavior as those who have and continue to get rich off of our uniqueness. So of course it's no surprise that Bill Cosby was applauded by some, booed by others, and ignored by the rest of us when he challenged Black folks to get it together. Nobody wants to hear that s**t right? Wrong. We want to hear it, but we want it to taste great too, just like our ribs ... Truth is, hearing about ourselves *from* ourselves is one of the most important ways for us to move forward. And I don't just mean when we reach seventy-five on the porch with our grandchildren. The way I see it, these are the last days. But they've been the last days for every generation throughout history. It was the last days for the Native Indians of North America when they got "jerked" for New York wasn't it? And it will really be the last days for us and our descendants if we don't get a grip on things real soon. Me? Well I'm a sucker for love I suppose. That's why I wish life was as simple as it appeared to be on the *Cosby Show*, with Cliff and Camille waltzing from the kitchen to the living room to the jazzy trumpet of Louis Armstrong and Dizzy Gillespie. And for some of us it is, to be fair. Success is hardly new to us as a people. But at this point, many of us have either never even heard of Satchmo, Dizzy, Bird or Monk, or simply could care less. For most they are just distant faces on dusty album covers in our peoples' old record collection. And so it is no surprise that we're now left waltzing to the cool, safe, groovy, watered down sounds of smooth jazz.

There was a time the stars were our only road map. Unfortunately most of you no longer even look at them at night. You used to use them for directions. The birds still head south for the winter as one flock though. How do they know where they're going? It's their nature. Pretty much all animals of a kind eat, drink, sleep, and work together. Black people are the exception. And it's a shame because we have so much to offer. We've always been multi-cultural, multi-lingual, and multi-talented people, from our roots in Africa to our current residence here in the West. That's right. But what is culture really? Is it language, music, food, body language, religious customs? Of course. It is all these things and more. But there is also one more thing culture is; YOU!!! Uh huh, everything you do, say, eat, drink, how you walk and talk is culture regardless of your so-called place of birth or current address. Yes you my brotha. But you probably never learned that in school, and chances are you didn't learn it at home either. But it's true. It's also true that we spoke different languages and dialects, wore different colors and fabrics, but we always had one thing in common. We were always unified in *spirit* and connected by a higher vibration. And we still are. As you know however, Africa no longer holds much cultural significance to the vast majority of Black folks in this country in this day and age. You'd be surprised at how quickly many so-called African-Americans will let you know real quick; "I am *not* like them people over there in Africa!" But when you ask them "Who were you *before* they brought you here they're suddenly at a loss for words. If only we realized that we were, and still are ONE, yet incredibly unique in every sense of the word there's no telling how high we could fly. When you dig deeper you realize that no two of us are identically alike, either in the physical sense, or genetically speaking. But we all belong to the same extended human family. Which makes it all the more perplexing why we are constantly in competition with one another over toys and trinkets which have absolutely nothing to do with what's really goin' on INSIDE. And all this does is keep us from getting to truly know one another on any kind of more meaningful level.

ONE STEP FORWARD ...

Whatever happened to Black Power? That's the first question. We sure know what white power is. Yes we do. As much as we faithfully support, maintain and sustain it mentally, physically, emotionally and

ECONOMICALLY we know white power like the back of our hand. If you could purchase power Lord knows we (Black folks) would all have it, as much as we consume. But brothers and sisters there really was a time when the words Black and Power occupied the same space. There was a period (late 60's and early to mid 70's) where African people (here and abroad) were embracing a different level of consciousness, cultural awareness and pride. From what they tell me we called each other brother and sister not dog and female dog! I don't think you heard me. I said we called each other BROTHER AND SISTER, not DOG AND FEMALE DOG!! During this era Black Power was in the minds and hearts of some of our boldest and brightest sisters and brothers. Even the term itself, Black Power conjures up a distinct image of tough looking brothers and sisters with blow out afros wearing leather jackets, berets and dark shades and toting big guns. This movement was in stark contrast to the Harlem Renaissance, Civil Rights and Pan-African movements of the 40's, 50's and 60's. But there was a common thread that linked these movements together aside from the amazing courage the men and women exhibited in the face of all kinds of resistance. I'm talking about the desire for CHANGE. See, what we Black folks really want (and have always yearned for) is change. Deep down inside this is what we yearn for. Problem is we have yet to define exactly what change actually *means*, and more importantly how to affect it. Secondly we haven't the slightest clue where to start. In other words, what are we fighting *for*? In the Civil Rights period it was equal rights and integration. The Pan-African theme was liberation and repatriation (both mental and physical) of Africans across the globe. And the Panthers advocated justice, the right to bear arms, decent homes and free breakfast programs for the youth. But what do we want today? Better yet, what as a people do we NEED? Just a question. Anyway, following all of this came the Afro-American "honeymoon" period of the early 80's where we found ourselves shaking off the scrapes and scars of the previous struggles. That's when the Big C hit. Yes my friends, Crack. The little white BOULDER came down so hard (in Black cities especially) at this time that twenty years later many of you are still trying to get your legs back. Not to say that the pipe didn't affect other segments of the population but for whatever reason we were "rocked" disproportionately. And this did much more to set us back than segregation ever did! And I mean generations. But we still kept trudging on. 1987 to the early 90's was a very unique time where you saw a resurgence and renewed interest in African culture, heritage and pride amongst Blacks. At least that's what it looked like. You began seeing more African attire, kente cloth, cowrie shells and cultural hairstyles (cornrows, braids, dreadlocks) sported by sisters and brothers all over the place. T-shirts with slogans such as "It's a Black Thing, You Wouldn't Understand" and "Fight the Power" began popping up on historically Black college campuses throughout the country. But it wasn't long before you also began to see the early stages of what we see in alarming abundance today. Young (and old) women proudly donning silky, luxurious, "European" looking hair weaves and extensions in place of their natural, beautiful, kinky and yes "nappy" heads. Doesn't it seem like we just keep taking one step forward only to take a couple more back? I mean, we all want to fit in somewhere it's true. But why must we be the ones to always compromise or sacrifice our own uniqueness in order to do so? That's a tough one to answer. But the numerous images plastered everywhere we turn, from the mall to the wall of your lady's hair salon don't make it any easier. No my friends, Black Power is all but a distant memory in the minds of most at this point. Instead what you see is Black folks embracing white power. And a bunch of misguided Negroes begging for reparations. When you take a closer look, Black Power failed for a number of reasons. For one, it's leaders failed to successfully incorporate the most powerful asset we bring to the table, our spirituality. And I'm not talking about religion, as was the platform for Martin and Malcolm. I mean our inherent spiritual link to the Creator and each other. There were politically motivated reasons that contributed to the demise of the Black Power Movement as well. And many forces working overtime to divide and conquer us mentally and physically. Still I wonder what might have been. I also wonder what the next movement will represent for Black folks. What thoughts, ideas, and action will drive it? And will we ever, for once and for all finally reach our destination? Whatchu think?

THREE PLACES AT ONCE

"I think you done lost your cotton pickin' mind that's what I think!" Just what I thought you'd say. Well then maybe you can explain how individually we are able to achieve practically any and everything on this Earth but collectively next to nothing? Big houses, beautiful cars, two weeks out of fifty two for vacation, Super Bowl rings, Nobel Peace Prizes, Oscars and the like but still mistrust and degrade each other so much that it's even hard to greet each other on the street! It's like this. Being Black (especially in America) requires you to develop a thick skin for "protection." We're encouraged to walk and chew gum at the same time then told "Don't you know you can't walk and chew gum at the same time??" The masks and disguises we don for the sake of fitting in are too numerous to mention here. But the fact remains that we change according to the particular situation we happen to find ourselves in. So whether it's the job interview, business lunch or Christmas party we dress, talk, and act like we've been trained in order to get what we want just like the creatures of habit we are. "Congratulations and welcome to the team!" "This is a fantastic company!" You're really gonna love it here." "Oh, just one more thing though brother; don't forget to shave your face okay?" And there you have it. What I'm really tryin' to say folks is, living this life has left us in tight jeans, hair weaves, bow-ties and muscle shirts. On the other hand, trying to "buck" the system can be as hazardous to your health as the cancer sticks you suck down during your fifteen minute break. But it ain't all bad. Not entirely. I mean, being Black in America does have it's privileges. But we'll get to those a bit later. For now just ask yourselves if bouncing up and down on this three places at once trampoline is really worth the trade-off.

Bottom Line: There are too many forces fighting against Black QUALITY, both inside and outside the Black community. As for how Black you are/aren't, well that is up to you to determine when nobody else is looking. For now just recognize your own unique gifts and talents and share them with others. Sounds simple doesn't it? Well that's just the start. Remember there is much more knowledge to be gained from your natural surroundings than any computer screen/program. By the way, wanna know what really happened to Black Power? Oh that's easy. You gave it away. Simple as that. Now get it back. 'Cause when it's all said and done it really doesn't matter where you come from at all. The real question is "Where y'all at?"

2

RED, BLACK AND BLUE

So here we are folks. Stuck between words/worlds, reality and the American Dream. When it comes to our curious fascination with this dream we seem to be more willing now than ever to compromise practically everything but the kitchen sink to attain it. So if that means stepping on a few toes along the way to reach "the top," eight times out of ten we're all for it. But don't you find this a bit odd, especially considering our well documented journey to these shores? I don't. In fact I see exactly why we yearn so much for the milk and honey this land promises. As a Black man immersed in the dream state for a good portion of my life I've been fortunate enough to experience the good, bad, ugly and downright crazy that America has to offer. I've felt the love, the pain, the smiles and cries of my people and the struggles we face each day to fit into a society that in many ways still considers us second and third class citizens (if that). If you were born in another country and emigrated to this country in pursuit of the dream chances are you will be considered more of an alien than E.T. See, there are varying degrees of the American Dream we continue to bathe, shampoo and condition ourselves in each and every morning. So it is no surprise that Dove, Dial, Coast, Safeguard and all the rest have become our cleansers of choice. We've been lathering up with them for so long that most of us believe they are the only ones that exist! Truth is, we're confused. And a lot of us just haven't made up our minds as to whether we want this American Dream, Dr.

King's Dream or just a big house in the suburbs. Anything but a Black Dream. By now we're well aware of the fact that the American Dream and King's were never the same. America's dream is enticing, invigorating, refreshing, and "Zestfully" clean. King's dream got him shot through the back of the neck on a balcony in Memphis, while achieving the American Dream could make you rich beyond your wildest imagination. The fulfillment of King's dream would surely make the world a better place, but at this point not even John Lennon could imagine that. Hard but true. So while we continue sleeping (and snoring), every MLK Jr. Boulevard from D.C to Detroit still looks exactly the same. Rundown, drug/liquor store infested, lined with check cashing joints, pawn shops and churches. Strangely enough, from the outside looking in anything and everything still seems attainable in America. And it is this hope that attracts the world's poor, tired, and huddled masses to see if all they've heard is true. Unfortunately not all are exactly welcomed to her shores with open arms to try their luck at the 'ol wheel of fortune. Just ask the Haitians … Still, the opportunity to obtain material wealth, fortune and fame is enough to make fathers leave their birth place and cross the border to join the "melting pot." Ironically, this same dream has daughters sliding down poles and dancing on tables for ones, fives, tens, and twenties. To be fair America affords you (its citizens) the same opportunity to succeed or fail depending on your consciousness and work ethic. But you also learn many hard lessons along the way. Valuable lessons like "It's not what you know but *who* you know," "It's all about the Benjamins baby," and "Only the strong survive." On the other hand where else could a young Black girl raised in poverty in Mississippi grow up to be the richest and arguably most powerful woman on the planet? Or a former bodybuilder and Hollywood action hero with zero political experience become governor of California overnight? You got it, America the Beautiful. The success stories are endless. The not so happy endings never make front page headlines. For instance there are countless Black men and women who served this country bravely and courageously in the military. In many cases they fought (and gave their lives) in the name of America even when they could not even eat in the same restaurants as whites just because of the color of their skin. Some are doing well. Others are struggling. That's because it is easy to become just another "number" or statistic around these parts. It happens every day. Meanwhile the VA hospital is filled with Black folks who joined the service to "Be all that they could be." Apparently not all dreams come true.

Nevertheless, in America there are as many "get rich quick" schemes as there are fish in the sea. Just make sure you know how to swim. Unfortunately most of the brothers and sisters I know don't get to the beach much these days. And the minute you do get a break from the hustle and bustle you're probably headed to where the sun shines a little brighter and the water sparkles a bit clearer than over here if you dig what I'm sayin.' But come one come all! It goes a little something like this. In America the running theme is "Life would be better somehow if I had this, that, or the other." The system's middle name is "Never Enough." So whether you've got eight million dollars in your pocket it's always cool to go for, say TWENTY! What's more confusing to the uninitiated is the fact that America and the United States are not the same thing. This is very important in understanding the puzzling dilemma she currently finds herself in. The Commander in Chief is called the President of the United States not the President of America for a reason. America, you see consists of signs and symbols, rumors, innuendo, burgers, fries, milkshakes etc ... In other words, it's basically just an idea. And as you know there are many Americas in existence. Unfortunately my friends, the United States at this point ain't one of 'em. A blind man can see that this country is more DIVIDED now than ever before, whether along racial, political or economic lines. Here you're either pro-war or pro-peace, pro-life or pro-choice, liberal or conservative etc ... So for all the talk of being united and such, division is openly encouraged and promoted in America. It keeps us off balance. The question remains; where exactly do you fit within the puzzle? Secondly, is it even possible to achieve the dream that is being hustled to you everywhere you turn? Is it even worth the effort? If you watch PBS you know that EVERYONE out here is from Africa. You do know that right? You also know ain't no way in hell you're going back to no damn Africa either! And why would you when the only picture you've seen all your life of the Motherland is the one with babies' ribs stickin' out of their chest with flies buzzing all over their faces? I mean seriously brothers and sisters! Is this *all* there is on the continent? I doubt it. But of course that's all you see. Alongside corruption, genocide and disease. Which in turn is all you end up believing. So now you've bought hook, line, and sinker the idea that Africa is completely a lost cause. Right? RIGHT BROTHA?? And so in some warped way we truly believe we (like other immigrants) actually came to America looking for a better way of life. I mean, weren't we doing just fine at HOME? Hmm … Anyway, these days you're lucky if you get the opportunity to even leave the country, much less get back to wherever it is you call home. So that leaves you with a few options: 1) Grit your teeth, roll up your sleeves and join the party. 2) Head up into the countryside, build yourself a cabin and live off the land. 3) Or get with it and start your own damn REVOLUTION! That's right, make some serious changes. "But how can I change things?" Where do I start?" That's up to you. Just know that door number three could be your ticket to freedom. Besides, what do you really have to lose anyway?

With that in mind, the fact remains that if you work hard and play by the rules you can achieve anything in this country. And with a little luck, once you've finally "made it" you're pretty much in the driver's seat. What they don't tell you is that the further you climb up the ladder the more the rules change. For example, I know plenty of brothers and sisters who work from sun up to sun down yet still have a hard time even making ends meet. Some of them languish in "low level" positions for minimum wages just to keep the lights on and water hot. Others put in eighteen hour days just to maintain their image and standard of living. So you see it's a trade-off. Sacrifice the majority of your time and energy and maybe, just maybe you can get yourself a house, clean ride and a few toys in your name. But what's the alternative?

Here's one. Tangie wants to be a nurse. It's all she ever talks about. She's wanted to be a nurse ever since she was a little girl. There's only one problem. Tangie can't afford college, rent, food, transportation plus living expenses. She comes from a small town in Colorado but now finds herself alone in a big, new city trying to figure out how to make her dreams come true and ends meet at the same time. Meanwhile her money is evaporating faster than she can say financial aid (which she is ineligible for). But Tangie is determined to make it and will do whatever it takes to get closer to the E.R. So she weighs her options and realizes she has just a few. 1) Work full-time during the day and attend school at night. 2) Sit out another year and reapply in the fall. 3) Head down to the local "gentlemen's club" and apply for a dancing position. Oh, and 4) Join the military. It's a tough decision for her to have to make, especially considering her conservative background and upbringing. But she feels that the only way she can accomplish her goals is if she has steady cash flow and time to study and attend labs. So she decides to do the "right thing," find a full-time job and go to school at night. But after a few weeks of "dead end" job hunting she reluctantly changes her mind and promises herself; "Only till I have enough money to pay for school and to live." Needless to say, the months pass, and Tangie is making more money than she's ever seen before. And predictably her priorities have now changed. Instead of attending labs she's now at the mall treating herself to lingerie from Victoria's Secret. Meanwhile it's getting harder and harder for her to concentrate on class when she's bringin' in enough bread to afford anything her heart desires. And all she ever wanted all her life was to be a nurse. So you see, attaining the American Dream ain't always all it's cracked up to be. And many well intentioned folks get swallowed up in the process. But a good number, Black, white or other actually do achieve it in one way or another even if it's not exactly the way they planned it.

One thing's for sure. There's nothing quite like winning. And no feeling more deflating than losing. Especially in America. If you've ever played competitive sports you know the difference. For Black people it's always been US vs. THEM. And for white people it's quickly become THEM vs. US. Herein lies the tug of war. America puts its winners on a pedestal, gives them a "free ride," ticker tape parade and invites them to the White House Lawn to play catch with the President. If you want these perks and much, much more second place is not an option. Did you ever see John Wayne, the Lone Ranger, Superman or Dirty Harry come in second? Hell no! Slogans such as "Winning isn't everything, it's the *only* thing" are cemented firmly in popular culture to such an extent that second place is about as desirable as secondhand smoke. And the current status of the Dream? Well let's just say that more Americans vote for American "idols" than they do to elect a new president. Furthermore, rappers are now household names whereas just twenty years ago the music was given less respect than disco. And the machine keeps rolling on. For those of you who don't know, it's all about PRODUCT around these parts. Whether in the form of rock n' roll, fast food/cars/women it's all the same. It has to do with perception. See, wherever you go outside of the States the image of America still is based on having "things." And this reputation (true or false) continues to suck people into her vortex. If you want to experience the finer things in life firsthand you know where to go. On the other hand, if you live in America you never truly realize how insulated you are until you travel elsewhere. For instance, many of you learned the Metric System of weights and measures early on in grade school. But due to the fact this system is rarely, if ever used in the States you probably disregarded it as out of date or useless. However, a simple trip practically anywhere else will show you how much of a minority you are on a global scale as you walk the streets with your book of conversions in your back pocket. So what's really the payoff for placing a "Golden Arches" in every corner of the globe? You already know. Mo' money, mo' power. But considering the fact that Lady Liberty became a "superpower" not even a hundred years ago, doesn't it seem a bit odd that today she has the whole world singing her song? Think about it. I'm still trying to figure out how Hawaii became the fifty second state! But aside from that, Black people still remain in limbo, infatuated by the American Dream yet becoming more and more comfortable with the American Nightmare. The difference between the two depends on how easily you can adapt.

"But we helped build this country!"

So did the Chinese, Japanese, Irish, Indian, Mexican, European, Jewish etc … That's not the point. The point is, as it's always been; who the hell are YOU Right now the game is wide open. You see the influx of various ethnic groups and cultures blending quite smoothly into the "machine" by following the blueprint, and these immigrants, "aliens," or whatever you wish to call them seem to understand this a bit more than the so called African-American. Which explains why you can walk into any Chinese, Arab or Indian convenience store/ take-out spot around the way and get your chicken wings, burgers, fries, rolling papers, incense, pre-paid phone cards and whatever else your heart desires. And why not, it's the American Way! But if you happen to be craving a pork chop sandwich or some curry chicken while you're walking through Chinatown you'll probably find your-self headed right back to good ol' MLK. See, we operate these businesses too, only we don't OWN them like the other ethnic groups. And they've just learned how to "flip the script" in order to make their own dreams come true. While we're on the subject of dreams, do you remember the last one you had? And if you don't mind me asking, did it come true?

"They do the jobs most Americans won't."

And if you happen to be up at five o'clock in the morning you'll usually see him perched in front of the corner store waiting to be scooped up by some business owner looking for "handymen" or day laborers. He is not a citizen. But he probably has a fake social security card/driver's license/green card. He works hard, doesn't complain and takes care of his business. Usually Mexican or from another Central or Latin American country, he personifies the new face of the American Dream. At least the face you see increasingly on television as the poster boy for immigration. Funny how you never see all the other ethnic groups who migrate to America (legally or otherwise) on CNN. Just these "brown" people. As you know, immigration/cheap labor has always been a staple of the American capitalist ideal. It also played a huge part in the construction and maintenance of this country. What scares people today about this "alien" is the fact that he (unlike the "African-American") could care less about integrating culturally with the rest of society. All he cares about is la familia. So in essence he is willing to play the game but has molded the rules to suit his individual as well as COLLECTIVE needs. We could learn a lot from "Jose." The fact that he has become so powerful (both economically and politically) in such a short period of time is a testament to his spirit and determination. Truth is, all ethnic groups have a vested interest in defining their position within the system. And the Brown man is as good an example as any to look to for inspiration.

"The only thing we have to fear is …"

Snakes? Heights? Being broke at 30? Being broke at 40? Failure, success? Anyway you slice it, FEAR is a b***h my friends, and the kind of thing that will either make you stand up or sit down. Most of the time we sit down, avoiding whatever it is that hits too close to home. "What if they don't like me?" Or "Everything depends on this!" There are people out here who are afraid to check their own mailbox!! Whether we admit it or not we're all afraid of something or other. And our fears elicit all types of unusual behavior like peeping through the blinds during the day or avoiding the city at night. Some of our fears have legitimate merit, but most are completely irrational. So what are *you* scared of? ... Fair question. We live in a world that is complicated. And if you watch the news you will see all types of crazy things that make you keep your eyes wide open. Truth is, mostly we are afraid of our own dreams. And this is why we make sure we forget them as soon as we wake up each morning. Our dreams frighten yet amaze us at the same time, especially the bad ones. So it's much easier to ignore them than to listen to what they're really trying to tell us. As I've said, Black people are dreaming. White people are dreaming. ALL of us are dreaming! For the so-called "African-American" the fear of a Black penis extends to our persistent and crippling mistrust of each other. It's paralyzing us as a people and preventing us from assuming our rightful position within (and without) the system. Many of us no longer even say hello to each other anymore, much less take the time to engage in any kind of meaningful communication. You see it on the street, in the supermarket, the workplace and the neighborhood. But it's impossible to sidestep the obvious. We're in PAIN y'all! Yes we are. Of course we play it off. That's just part of the gig. But when we're not "frontin" how do we process this pent up anger, rage, frustration and powerlessness we feel but keep inside? I'll tell you how, by avoiding how we really feel towards each other and finding every distraction under the sun to help keep our emotions under wraps that's how! You know it's true. Admitting that we're hurting in the first place implies weakness and none of us want to be seen as that. Reputation goes a long way in the business of Blackness, and copping to your fears could get you labeled all types of less than flattering names. But it affects every area of our lives from our most intimate relationships to our lack of collective unity. Hidden emotions, repressed feelings and strange behavior. This also explains how we can be so incredibly warm to one another one day and bitterly cold the next. See, it's much easier just to keep our dealings on a superficial level till the next time we meet. Still we have no problem pushing one another's buttons and dissecting each other's weaknesses whenever we decide our EGO needs nourishment. But what happens at the end of the day? The pain only gets worse and we still end up absorbing it ourselves, leaving us wondering why the hell we feel the way we do.

Maybe that's why everyone's doing yoga these days. And why we keep on buying things we can't afford. America has no problem with that whatsoever. No sir. She'll sell you things you don't need quicker than you can say blood diamond. In fact the "Web" is filled with sites where you can zone out and double click to your heart's desire. No need to re-enter your credit card information either, they know it by heart. There are many places you can go to retreat from the struggle and satisfy your every want and need. As for your future? ... Like I said, the Black man/woman in (and outside) America is at a serious crossroads. You can smell it in the air. And as time continues to disappear you begin to realize that some people's dreams really do come true while others fall to the wayside or simply get left behind. Maybe that's how the system was designed in the first place? Regardless, it is hard to watch the so called "African-American" as he morphs into a barely recognizable manikin still smarting from the whips and chains of brainwashing. Institutionalized? Of course! Self-induced? Yes, that too. Truth is, at this point we're basically afraid of our own shadows. Or should I say EXPECTATIONS. So what do we do? Lower them. And this is one of the most notorious areas in which the F.O.A.B.P rears its ugly "head." What happens is we sabotage/sacrifice our own individuality for the sake of fitting in, getting "paid" and so on and so forth. The world already is well versed on how INCREDIBLE you are brotha! And they've already let you know that they will clone, imitate and copy every tool you bring to the table just to show how much they admire your creative genius. The question is; how much of yourself are you willing to compromise in order to fit in? Meanwhile the fear continues to spawn a whole host of conditions ranging from depression, confusion, schizophrenia, minstrelsy and coonism to name just a few. And we've all been injected with different dosages and experienced multiple side effects. Unfortunately there is no specific date as to when the Black man/woman actually misplaced his/her true creative powers, it's been more of a gradual process. Fortunately there is a remedy. But we'll get to that later.

I'll tell you this though, Black people aren't the only ones feeling the pressure. America herself is sweatin' bullets and shaking like a leaf just waiting for the inevitable. See the world is expanding by leaps and bounds and soon she will be forced to join the playing field as it continues to level off. As you may or may not have noticed Lady Liberty is no longer the vivacious "supermodel" she once was. And if you look closely enough you can clearly see the stretch marks. Everyone else is catching up. On top of that she is getting *browner* than ever. It's true. This couldn't be what the founding founders had in mind could it? But dig this; a funny thing happens when you travel to other places in the world. You immediately notice a couple of things. 1) America's undeniable influence and magnetic allure and 2) What others think of her. And best believe they *always* have an opinion. Interestingly enough you can still pay with U.S currency anywhere you happen to touch down. But things are changing. If you've ever had a problem with your computer and were forced to call product support then you know what I'm talking about. Nine times out of ten the voice on the other end ain't gonna sound like "Jack" that's for damn sure. And this is making Americans uneasy. So now you start to hear things like "Why can't I talk to someone who speaks *English* for Christ's sake?" Or "I can't understand a word these people are saying!" Fear sure does cause a lot of strange behavior doesn't it? Indeed …

On the "Black hand side," America has a rich and well documented history of fearing the African "apparatus." On a side note, if I told you the number of times I've experienced this fear first hand you'd probably say I need therapy. WE ALL DO! But if you've ever walked into an elevator and felt (sensed) a Caucasian woman clutch her purse a bit tighter you know exactly what I'm talking about. Or maybe you were just trying to locate your vehicle in a crowded parking lot and heard the automatic door locks click as you passed by. I'm beginning to think I fit the damn description for every carjacking or purse snatching in the history of mankind! But let me calm down … We all know that castration, lynching, police brutality and identity theft are as much a part of this country's illustrious fabric as the Fourth of July. But what exactly is it about the Black "manhood" that is so threatening to the welfare and security of the powers that be? What are these people REALLY afraid of? Indeed, there must have been something profoundly unique or extraordinary about the Negroid's "package" that drove the founding fathers to go to such great lengths to attempt to destroy it. Let us for a moment examine this issue from a historical context. Throughout the "slave trade" it was regular practice of the European to cut off (mutilate) the genitals of the strongest most virile African as to promote fear and cause division amongst the rest of the clan. And this inferiority complex (whether real or imagined) has continued to manifest itself in all types of ways even today. The African, so called African-American as well as his brethren and sistren throughout the diaspora has weathered the most brutal forms of violence and degradation known to mankind. All in the name of power. In fact, power and the use/misuse of it are recurrent themes in this country. It is no secret that America has an infatuation with power. You see this everywhere in American society from the "field" of professional sports to the "big house" (White House). It is also no coincidence that smack dab in the center of this nation's capitol and seat of government power and influence, Washington, D.C stands the Washington Monument perpetually erect (and white) for the world to see. A lot of you may not know that this phallic symbol also has its origins in Egypt (which by the way still lies in Africa) despite the ridiculous attempts to move Egypt to the "Middle East" (wherever that is). But regardless of America's obvious fascination with, and imitation of the darker persuasion and our symbols, it seems as though it is still us who continue to exhaust our very last drop of energy trying to adopt hers! But not so fast.

ONLY IN AMERICA

The "Sweet Science" of boxing remains perhaps the most interesting example of the rags to riches, "ashy to classy" allure of the American Dream. And it is one of the only arenas where a Black man can be "cocky" and actually be applauded for it. We all are familiar with legendary promoter Don King flashing his million dollar smile and that tiny red, white and blue flag yelling "Only in America!, Only in America!!" as his fighters (predominantly Black and Hispanic) prepare to duke it out in the ring. They dish out and sustain brutal punishment for any number of rounds just to receive a bejeweled belt and "purse" for their troubles. If you have the skills, proper management and promotion you too could be a contender. And make no mistake the sleazy sport has produced some of the most memorable figures and personalities this country has ever seen. From the "Greatest" himself Muhammad Ali to the transformation of Big George Foreman from grizzly bear to grill guru/multi-millionaire there have been many colorful figures that have danced in an outside the ring. The fighter's tale has been told countless times from Jack Johnson to Sugar Ray Robinson and Joe Louis with the standard tragic ending. Broke, brain damaged and damn near penniless but considered a true warrior. "Hey Champ can I get your autograph?!" But even Ali has sold his own name for a dollar or couple hundred million. That *really* surprised me. But I ain't mad at my brother. Once again this is just another example of the American Dream realized. Yes, when it's all said and done, the boxing game usually leaves a bitter taste in the mouths of it's participants who spill their blood and guts inside the squared circle. But it's not that much different than many of us who take our share of bumps and bruises and end up looking for the ice pack. It is what it is. And there's always another "Great White Hope" waiting in the wings. Unfortunately he usually doesn't stand a chance against the "Champ." In baseball, there's three strikes and you're out.

In boxing if you're the challenger you usually only get one shot. Point is, we're all fascinated watching two Black men beating each other damn near to a pulp. Nothing seems to quite compare to the hype, tension and buildup to the big fight. In fact we plan huge gatherings around it. There's brew, Hennessey, chips, dip and whatever else you need to get your mind right. But only occasionally does the "main event" live up to the pre-fight hype and barber shop banter that precedes it. More times than not all you get is two brothas beatin' each other senseless till one gets awarded the decision or eventually knocked the f**k out! But once the house lights at Caesar's Palace come up and everyone heads home all you're left with is a few fond memories and "highlights" of everything that went down. And there you have it. One winner, one loser and two brothas "swolled up," woozy, punch drunk and of course, red, black and blue.

Bottom Line: As we go through life we all experience our share of bumps and bruises. The reality is that none of us, Black, white, red or purple are exempt. But it is how we respond to these challenges that defines our character and ultimately our success or failure in life. America is a great place to live if you have the courage to be true to yourself. If not, you will. That is, once you finally come to the realization that you have no other choice.

3

NAME THAT COON

So last week I finally got tired of being a nigger(a). Therefore I decided to go down to the courthouse and do a little somethin' about it. As I sat on the bus I found myself slowly drifting off, pondering my future and rambling to no one in particular; "What are you doin' man?" "Huh?" As I approached my stop I began to have second thoughts. But I decided to go for it anyway. So I calmly stepped off the bus and entered the courthouse with every intention of changing my name. Found out which line to stand in, took my number and waited. Couple minutes went by and I started thinking again. "Why are you really here dude?" "It's only a name!" "What's in a name anyway?" I mean, aren't the words we use to describe ourselves simply just that, *words*? What's really important is how we feel about ourselves inside and the way we treat one another ain't that right? I guess. But if you're Black and happen to have the name Tom (Thomas, Tommy, etc ...) then you might be the brunt of more than a few cruel jabs by your own brothas no less! But regardless of the name your Mama and Daddy chose for you as you entered this world, if you're anything like me at some point or another you've probably wondered what your *real* name would be had you not been raised here in the Wild Wild West. And no I'm not talkin' about the aliases you've so easily adapted to over the years. You know, like n***a, colored, Negro (niggrah), "Afro-American," "African-American," Black etc ... There are many others as well, but porch monkey, jungle bunny, spear chucker, coon, watermelon man and the rest are usually reserved for "special occasions." Let's just say we as brothers/brothas and sisters/sistas have more than enough nicknames to go around. And they all have different connotations in the Black as well as white world. That's why you go ballistic whenever a white person calls you the world famous N-word but take it as a warm greeting when Raheem calls you it. "S'up my n***a!" "What's happenin' man!" See, it's not the same thing folks. IT'S JUST NOT! However this is very hard to explain unless you're hip to the jive. It can't be explained intellectually. It's more like a feeling you get inside when referring to your man like "Oh yeah that's my n***a right there!" Like a term of endearment if you can understand where I'm comin' from. What I can't understand is how, like clockwork every fifteen, twenty years or so I find myself having to wrap my head around yet another name deemed appropriate for myself and those that look like me. It's like; "Wasn't the last one good enough?" I mean, at least they could do a poll or something before the next name change don't you think?

Anyway, let's talk about insecurity for a second people. As you know Black folks have been getting the "royal shaft" for centuries now. So much so that we've grown quite accustomed to and comfortable with it as time goes by. But this has created an interesting dilemma for us as we continue our quest for complete integration into the society at large. Why are we the only ones who have to constantly update (upgrade) our status within the American system? Let's start with the whole African-American situation. The term itself, "African-American" has come to mean anyone with African (Black) ancestry and American nationality. In other words, people of African descent (from the continent) who were sold to Europeans and forced into slave labor in North America even before there was a place called U.S.A. But what does the term really suggest? It's almost like throw half of one and half the other together and presto, now you have the so-called "African-American." And although there are many Americas that exist in the Western Hemisphere (Latin, Central, North, South,

Middle etc.) for some reason the name African-American usually only refers to Black people in the United States and not say, a "Latin" American country like Honduras. Why is that? It seems that these days the name has more to do with the Black CONDITION (position within the system) rather than any tangible historical ties to the Motherland. Millions of Africans landed in the West Indies and Central America throughout the course of the slave trade while a much smaller number were brought to North America and enslaved in the United States. But if you travel to any island in the Caribbean or South America today you will rarely ever see this hyphen attached to any other group. You do see it with Afro-Cuban for instance but this is just to describe an aspect of the culture (music, rhythms, dance). So-called "African-Americans" on the other hand have gotten quite cozy with the hyphen over the last twenty, thirty years or so. Or as Toni Morrison in her work, *Playing in the Dark, Whiteness and Literary Imagination* (1992) put it, "American means white, and Africanist people struggle to make the term applicable to themselves with ethnicity and hyphen after hyphen." She's right. The truth is, Black people in this country really have nothing else to remind us of our true nationality and origin on the continent of Africa, especially since we've adopted European forms and styles of dress and mannerisms. In other words, "Sista you don't know *where the hell you from*! And how could you considering the circumstances. So you see this leaves us with no real concept of HOME, though we are able to identify at least in some degree to wherever our parents' parents' parents' were brought to in slave ships. So it is no surprise why we seem a bit anxious now and then. We're homesick, point blank. After all, whether you're a schoolteacher, maintenance man, bus driver or attorney the first thing you wanna do after a long day at work is go home! Right? That's because home is the place in your heart you feel most comfortable. It's where you can walk around buck naked if that happens to be your cup of tea. Yet one thing many of us haven't come to terms with is our relationship to America and why it's still so hard for us to feel at ease. But Lord knows we keeps on tryin.' Regardless, even if you do that DNA search to uncover your true genealogy and roots on the continent something would still be missing. Not lost, but missing. It's tough y'all. You'd be surprised how few so-called African Americans even realize that Africa is a CONTINENT and not a country to begin with! But that's a whole 'nother story. More perplexing is how flexible we've become. As you know by now the so-called "African-American" has grown quite comfortable crashing with his "Uncle Sammy" while his birth Mama (Africa) is off dealing with her many issues. So for the sake of accuracy I would like to introduce a more appropriate name to describe the Black man/woman here in the twenty-first century. For the remainder of this text we'll call him the American-African, or "Amerfrican" for short. Cool? Cool. Meanwhile, our Caucasian American brothers and sisters who obviously migrated from the continent of Europe somehow became exempt from this hyphen hysteria and are simply called Americans, thereby avoiding the confusion and insecurity that comes with identity crises. For instance, there was a time when Negro was the primary term used to describe (define) us. There were some cats who were like "That's right jack!" I ain't your *brotha*! I ain't no colored. I'm a NEGRO! And don't you *ever* forget it!!!" Perhaps it seemed like an upgrade so we just ran with it. It wasn't quite "African," but far less of a derogatory vibration than nigger that's for sure. Anyway, over the years I've known many white boys who act "Black.". And it seems as though they've had no problem going along with the program either. "Yo yo yo, what up nig!" "What's poppin' my nigga? First time I heard it I was kinda shocked to be honest. Then it dawned on me that white people are more comfortable with the word than even we are! After all, they have been using it longer than we have. Marinate on that for a sec ... But for real, check this out. I have a Caucasian buddy who was born and raised in South Africa and has been in the States attending university. He loves America and is even considering making it his "home" after graduation. Hearing him speak, the last place on Earth you would say he was from would be the Motherland. Yet, "technically" he is more African-American than the majority of you handkerchief head Negroes! Sorry … Seriously though, I wonder what he'd think of actually being called African-American? Next time I see him I'll ask him. In the meantime my friends you see how this name game business has more to do with our current condition of suspended animation here in America than we care to admit. What's even more intriguing is the fact that you don't even have to squint to clearly see the direct physical resemblance between our brothers and sisters in Africa and here in America. But you also see how confusing the name game can get if you play it long enough. I'm beginning to think the hyphen is really some sort of badge of honor to remind us how far we've come (or not). Or perhaps it's just another Black thing I wouldn't understand. One thing's for certain. What we call ourselves, and more importantly why has a lot more to do with *how* we see ourselves than we think.

"Whaddup dawg?"

Each morning I try to get in a workout to start the day off. The other day I was warming up and happened to notice a couple of ladies walking their dog not too far from me. Handsome enough looking pup with a shiny coat and huge paws. Looked like a Black Labrador, pure breed. I watched curiously as the women began barking out commands to the puppy as they worked on training him. "INKY, SIT!" "HEEL BOY!" "LAY DOWN!" Every time the dog obeyed the commands he was rewarded with a little treat. "Good dog Inky, good dog." This must've gone on for ten more minutes or so as I did my jumping jacks. Watching Inky being "trained," I couldn't help but draw a comparison to the conditioning of Black people in America from the time we were brought over here. And how at the present time we've literally become "dogs" to each other, obediently answering to this absurd term of apparent endearment. Look here folks. Slang and disrespect ain't the same thing! Understand? But how often have you tossed around this "dog" greeting like a Nerf football between father and son on a breezy Sunday afternoon? It's so common these days that its freely used as much by my white, yellow, brown and red brothers as it is by my Black dogs. Kinda like nigga. But DOG?? C'mon man! Apparently it's the new Hello, surfacing sometime around 1993 or'94, tracking dirt inside the house, barking at all the neighbors and plopping itself right beside you on the couch. Remember how the old folks used to say; "You run around with dogs you're bound to catch fleas!" Makes me wonder what's coming next. So now you even have women cosigning this madness talking about "Chile you know ain't no good men out here. They all *dogs*!" Wow ... As far as my government name (the one that appears on my driver's license, birth certificate, social security card, paycheck) that's only good for when I'm traveling, interviewing for a job or happen to get in a little hot water if you know what I'm sayin.' Other than that it's every other nickname you could think of. Be that as it may, for now let's just focus on the role your name(s) plays in your growth, development and maturation. And how as a people these names have become as ingrained in our community as the drive-thru.

THE MIRROR SIDESTEP

Your name defines you and gives you a sense of self. Therefore it should reflect that which makes you *you*. In fact, anything that you respond to or repeat literally hundreds of times a week carries a certain vibration and frequency you absorb and internalize. Unfortunately though, like I've said the majority of us carry names around which we haven't the slightest relation to anything we represent. Names such as Williams, Smith, Johnson and Thompson which we wear with pride but have no relation whatsoever to our heritage, lineage, culture, etc ... And this simply adds to the slippery search for our true nature and identity that we all yearn for but rarely actively seek. When you look at yourself in the mirror in the morning it is your own reflection staring back at you. When you sign your name on the dotted line you get the name of whoever held your ancestors captive. This is true. We live in a day and age when our own parents can't tell us where the family name came from. Don't believe me though,

ASK THEM! They will tell you just that; "I don't know baby." Either that or "Honey, there's more important things to worry about than that nonsense." But if you do even the smallest bit of research into the origin of either one of your names you would find that nine times out of ten both originate in a land far, far away, and most likely someplace in Europe. So now many of us attempt to reconnect with our African root by creating names from the furthest regions of our vivid imaginations. I have friends with such colorful first names as Ledravian, Shandrika, and Starling. Straight up. Many more of my Muslim brothers and sisters adopt Islamic names to signify their faith, which I think is great. Fortunately it's really quite easy to find out what your name actually means and its origins. Simply do a Google search. Insert your first name and see what comes up. Do the same for your last name (and middle if you have one). You'll probably be surprised at the results. But the real disconnect comes in not knowing exactly how you arrived at receiving it. I wish I knew. But for most of you it's not even an afterthought. This is a very strange phenomenon indeed. True story; I was watching a sporting event not too long ago and was listening to the commentators on the play by play. This brother was doing the on-field commentary. Although I didn't recognize him by name, he appeared to be an ex-athlete. He was also "Black as night." So after a particularly spectacular play, the brother expertly broke it down from a player's perspective and sent it back up to the booth with "This is John Jones givin' you the bird's eye view. "Now back up to you guys in the studio …" Right then and there I straightened up on the couch, scratched my head like, JOHN JONES! You don't even *look* like a Jones brotha! I mean g**damn!!! As Black as you are you look like a Lumumba or Kenyatta or something. Anything but John Jones!!! Then I remembered that day I myself had gone down to the courthouse with the direct intention of changing my name to something more "African" but left without even filling out the necessary paperwork!!! And how I justified leaving by asking myself; "What difference does it make anyway?"

Remember *Roots?* That incredibly vivid 70's miniseries that put a face on slavery and eventually becoming the highest rated series of it's kind in the history of television? Alex Haley's epic educated the masses about slavery's impact on the Black psyche, community and family tree. I remember as a small child myself being glued to the television entranced by the horrific images I saw before me. Shocked yet fascinated by what I was watching, *Roots* made me see things in an entirely different way. There was one scene in particular that stayed with me for many, many years. You probably remember it well yourself, it's the one where the Europeans are attempting to break down the Africans' will in order to make them less rebellious and easier to enslave. A young African named Kunta, chained and shackled from head to toe refuses to be "broken" despite the repeated attempts of the European to destroy his spirit. "What is yer name boy?" the white man yells nastily. "Kunta!" he responds despite the vicious lashes from the white man's whip. "Boy, I say what is yer name?" "KUNTA!" "No, your name is Toby! Now SAY IT!! More lashes … "My name … is Kunta!" Whap Whap!!! "YOUR NAME IS TOBY!" "SAY IT!!!" Lash after lash until this proud African, bloody, battered and nearly unconscious finally submits to the bull whip and responds with a barely audible whisper; "My name … is … Toby …" Remember that? I sure do. I also remember when we used to sit down and eat together at the dinner table each night.

So the other day I happened to run into an old friend I hadn't seen since college. It was at the mall. I didn't even recognize her at first. Matter of fact, it was her that recognized me. So anyway, first it was the "Hey, don't I know you from somewhere?" kinda awkward moment you get when you can't put a name to a face. I tried for the life of me to remember her but it just wasn't happenin.' She remembered mine though, which was kinda cool I must admit. So after a couple minutes of playing catch up and "Where Are They Now?", I finally broke down and said; "I'm sorry sister but what was your name again? She smiled easily and replied; Hiari. So of course I was like

"Hiari," what a pretty name, I've never heard that before. Then I was really stumped as to who she was. She cut me off me as if she knew exactly what I was thinking with; "You probably remember me as Jennifer. That's when the face and name clicked and I was like *Jenny*!!! I wish I'd a seen the look on my face for that one! She sure did look a lot different than I remember from school that's for sure. Then again don't we all? Maybe it was the locks she now sported or the kente cloth dress she wore. But now that I think about it what I remember most was her "new" name, Hiari. I asked her what it meant and she said with the same smile and the proudest look on her face; "It means Free Will." All I could say was "Go 'head Sista …!"

Bottom Line: It's not even really about a name people. It's about an IDENTITY, although I must say I wish I had a cool nickname growing up. Something like Clyde or Ice. Yeah *Ice*. Many of my childhood friends had funny ones like Goose, Moose, Frog and Bird. But I wanted something that sounded *cool*. In most cases your nickname says more about you than the first name your parents choose for you. This is because usually your given name is selected mainly because it sounds good whereas your nickname actually "fits" or describes a unique quality YOU possess. Plus you can trace it back to who originally gave it to you and why. More importantly, there are feelings or emotional connections to nicknames that rarely come with given names. In fact I have friends to this day that I couldn't tell you what their born name was, only what everybody calls them. Ironically, people wear their nicknames with pride and can run down the "science" and history behind them in the blink of an eye. Ask them what their born name means and they just may have to do that Google Search. One last thing to think about; the ONLY reason you have your family name is because somewhere down the line one of your ancestors decided to take on the name of the "slave master" who enslaved him. Point blank. Simple as that. No other reason. So with that in mind, brotha what'd you say your name was again?

4

THE RACE CARD

By now we've all heard the story of the Indians discovering a scruffy, frail looking young man in 1492 wandering aimlessly across the ocean and approaching their shores obviously lost and unsure of his whereabouts. The sight of this odd looking creature undoubtedly startled them having lived there for hundreds, if not thousands of years. Nevertheless they welcomed him and his shipmates with open arms into their villages, fed them, showed them the lay of the land, gave them a hot meal etc ... We all know what happened next. Fast forward to the year 2000. Let's say you live in Senegal and you've got some vacation time coming and decide to visit the good 'ol United States just to see what all the fuss is about. You probably speak a fair amount of English, hopefully enough to make your trip a bit easier. You're undoubtedly excited and curious to find out if all you've heard is true and eager to get the most out of your trip to the States. So naturally you decide to spend the first part of your trip visiting the usual landmarks (Washington Monument, Ellis Island, Times Square). But after a few days of sightseeing you're ready to visit the land of the first "American" tribes and check out *their* "monuments." But soon you become surprised and thoroughly disappointed upon finding out these Natives have been relocated, for lack of a better word. And for the most part they now live on plots of land completely isolated from the rest of society called reservations. And since you are unfortunately not invited to a pow-wow you end up returning to your homeland without a hint of evidence much less a souvenir showing these indigenous peoples ever even existed! In fact, here in the twenty-first century it seems as if the only way to catch even the faintest glimpse of an indigenous "American" is to either visit a reservation or be in the mood for some Blackjack. How is this possible? I mean, shouldn't a picture of a Brown man be the first thing that comes to mind when you think of an American? And even *they* came from somewhere else! But all this is just my way of saying "Something just ain't right people." There are British folks who agree. And they too celebrate Thanksgiving, albeit for different reasons than Sarah, Bradley, and Tyrone. They're like; "I'm sure glad those wankers left jolly ol' England and went over there to settle!" "We didn't want them over here anyway!" "Good riddance!!" Which leads me to my next question brothers and sisters: What do Indians (Native Americans) do for Thanksgiving? Answer: The same thing *you* do on the 4th of July brotha. Numb the pain.

But check this out. I was in the supermarket not too long ago in the checkout line standing behind a very interesting looking cat. I tried my best not to stare at this dude with pale skin, "kinky" white hair, broad nose, thick lips and sky blue eyes but it was tough. When he opened his mouth it sounded like he had a German accent. Immediately I thought to myself; "what planet is this cat from?" "Wonder what *he* has to go through on a daily basis." But then I thought "What does this man consider himself racially?" Black, white, mulatto, albino? I was about to ask him but decided against it. He looked as if he was in a hurry anyway. But the image stayed with me for awhile and made me think about this whole thing we call race, or at least our narrow perception of it. And why it keeps coming up every time another bonehead shock jock forces us to discuss the role it plays in our everyday lives. Race (and its half-brother "Ism") for some reason seems to rub a lot of people the wrong way as if it is just a match waiting to be sparked. Most of you would rather just act like it (the tension) just doesn't exist. You constantly hear things like "Why can't you just let the past be the past?" Or "Why must you always play the race card?" whenever any racially charged incident or situation arises. But these are just smokescreens. And just where did our concept of race actually originate? Many of my religious brothers and sisters will say it comes from the Holy Bible and the breakdown (genealogy) of the tribes as depicted in the Good Book. Perhaps, but why then do we continue to let it color our outlook so much while our Caucasian brothers and sisters consider it nothing more than a convenient excuse? The truth is, white people don't think about race to the extent that Blacks do simply because they have no reason to. See, in America whiteness is like an all day bus pass. Or good credit. With A-1 credit there's no need for a co-signer (which eliminates many of you to begin with). What I'm trying to say is that thinking about what doesn't apply to you only complicates things. But denying that it even exists is dangerous. And we all know that race has more to do with color than anything else. Still I wonder if the French, Chinese and German knew what color they were when they first came to America? There's so much confusion out here these days when it comes to race that it probably is easier to claim that there's only one, the human race. But where does that leave my German albino brother when it comes time for him to fill out his job application? What is he supposed to check? Your guess is as good as mine.

In any event, we hear the word race so frequently and in so many different contexts it's almost grown a mind of its own. Look around you. It's clear the world is more divided along racial lines than ever before. In reference to us, the term distinguishes one population of an animal species (including human) from another of the same subspecies, usually by certain physical traits such as skin color, facial features, hair texture, genes, and self-identification. Today we identify race more so with ethnic groups than anything else. And in order to classify and categorize we tend to use stereotypes as our Seeing Eye dog. When the European "explorers" were busy invading other nations in their quest for world supremacy they encountered a puzzling dilemma. Everywhere they sailed they ran into men and women that looked completely different than them in size, stature, behavior, language, and most importantly COLOR. You can imagine how paranoid they must have been when they realized that the world was not only round but a much darker place than they had envisioned, especially just emerging from the Dark Ages themselves. So they came up with various categories to document these physical attributes and cultural differences between people. At some point they began to equate these characteristics and behavioral qualities with intelligence (or lack thereof) and mental capacity. It's like this. First of all, man fears what he can't understand. This is as true today as it was during the days of Columbus and his crew. However, over time even this concept of race changed and became simply another word in the English language to have multiple meanings, kinda like the word WHEN. In one context WHEN can mean "Back in the day WHEN we used to be unified." But in the next breath it could also mean "I can't do nothin' for you brotha, but WHEN you get back on your feet holla at me!" That's the thing about the English language, the same word changes shape and form and transcends time and space depending on how it's used. Other words are interchangeable as well like "hot" and "cool." So we come to this slippery thing called race, and what it means to the Amerfrican. There are many races in this country; Rat race, Senate race, "New York City Marathon," Kentucky Derby. And we know that race in the United States is not the same as race in say ... Brazil for instance. In America, we also know that this little word race in conjunction with it's baby 'bro "ism" has caused men to commit some of the most dastardly deeds imaginable, incited riots, and helped shape the very world we now live in.

RACISM

When you think about how ridiculous it is to discriminate against another person just because they're skin is a different color than yours it makes you wonder what's really going on beneath the surface. A lot of you feel that only white people are capable of being racists. I disagree. You don't have to have KKK tattooed on the back of your neck to despise your brother. All it takes is a little ignorance and a few shots of Jack (or Patron). And stereotypes come in all shapes, sizes and colors man. Which begs the question; is it possible to be TOO BLACK? Hmm … I do know that although it has always been okay for Brad to drink from my water fountain it is also possible for me to discriminate against him because of his pale features. And I must admit there are more than a couple "cracka" jokes in my vocabulary. But there's also a thing called home training that runs through my bloodstream. And I've always prided myself on being more warm-hearted than mean-spirited anyway. So like many of you, there are countless times I find myself thinking one thing yet keeping my true feelings to myself. I'm sure it has something to do with the way I was raised. Regardless, racism is not something that just falls from the sky into your living room folks. Nor is it simply an attitude. And it doesn't always involve being beaten senseless over the head with batons, sicced on by German shepherds or chased out of redneck diners either. It is an acquired taste, taught from father to son, mother to daughter, uncle to nephew. But sadly it is also self-perpetuating. There are folks (white and Black) that would love your last image of James Brown (R.I.P) to be his freaky looking mug shot! We're talking about the Godfather of Soul here!! So you see the racism that we preach against yet still practice today is slippery to say the least. For instance, I only watch golf when Tiger Woods is playing. Does that make me racist too? Hard to say, but we've embraced this concept, perhaps not to the same degree as our Caucasian brothers and sisters but to the particular level which suits us. Oh I'm sure many of you beautiful brothas and sistas right now are like "N***a please!" "I *know* I ain't no racist!" "I don't control no institutions, don't bring the guns or drugs into the neighborhood." "And I damn sure spend my money with white folks!" Indeed you do sista … "Besides, you need to be in power to be a racist." "And who makes the laws huh?" "Not us!" You're right honey. Sort of. Racism does involve power and the misuse of it. But not the kind of power that you think. Twenty years ago Black people had more "power" than we do even today. Consider this; at one point the "Gloved One" was the number one pop star on the planet, #23 was the best basketball player in the universe, "Iron Mike" was the heavyweight champion of the world, Eddie the hottest actor in Hollywood, "the 'Cos" had the number one rated show on television, Carl Lewis was the fastest man on Earth, Jesse was considered the first serious Black candidate for president, and Ms. Winfrey was well on her way to conquering the entire free world. WOW!! Remember that? All incredible accomplishments indeed, but this demonstrates only one aspect of power, economic. There are many forms of power my friends, the most important of which is personal. And the misuse of this power is what's responsible for much of the racism out here today, most of which you never even notice. Like I said before, most of us underestimate the power and impact words alone have on our state of mind. But what happens when you tell a child she's brilliant vs. telling her she's stupid? So you see how even a single word can change a person's whole outlook. And racism goes far deeper than being insensitive or hurting someone else's feelings. Hell, we do that almost every day, sometimes unconsciously, most times on purpose.

"Yo Mama's so Black, when she puts on yellow lipstick, she looks like a cheeseburger."

Anything for a laugh right? Uh huh. Over the years we have been conditioned to believe that putting each other down is just all in good fun. But once again it comes down to how we process the pain. Even the funniest of Black comedians are simply trying to negate Amerfricans' pain through laughter. Unfortunately sometimes this too only heightens the discomfort. So instead of letting it go we internalize it even more and begin to dump it on each other. Then we repeat the jokes to whomever we believe it may concern. Truth is, we don't all love watermelon. Nor do all of us eat fried chicken (although we may be able to fry it better than *you)*. Not every cab driver wearing a turban has a bomb in his trunk either. But these days the line between respect and disrespect is virtually non-existent. Consequently, the insults, jabs and uppercuts we hurl at each other every chance we get reflect how we really feel about each other behind closed doors. The fact of the matter is these "one-liners" and "harmless" jokes affect us much more than we care to let on. When we're the quarterback of these darts it becomes "Aw man you know I was just playin!" "What, you can't take a joke?" Truth is, words hurt. If you've ever been called a "chink," "spic," "wop," "kike," "wetback," "cracka ass cracka," "sand nigger," or "jungle bunny" then you know what I mean. There really is no such thing as "friendly fire" when it comes to putting each other down. And as we all know from watching the nightly news patriot missiles kill the same as regular ones. So whether it's stand-up comedians, late night talk show hosts, rappers or our own brothers and sisters it's all the same. "Black people always late!" "Why, if it wasn't for free drinks before 11:00 you n***as wouldn't even make it to the club!" Ha ha very funny. And yet words also have the power to heal. Truth is we all perpetuate stereotypes towards our own particular ethnic group as well as others each and every day. Then we get bent out of shape when someone else airs out our "dirty laundry." Imagine that!

"White people love to act Black."

Yeah, till they realize that actin' Black and *livin'* Black are two entirely different things. Being Black has always been synonymous with being cool. But a white woman wouldn't dare come to work wearing an Afro wig or hair extensions. And if she did she would be laughed out of the office before she even had the chance to clock in. On the flip side, an Amerfrican female would not have a second thought going to work sporting a "weave" or straightened hair. Interesting. But consider this; what if Black men suddenly began straightening their hair and wearing colored contact lenses in order to look more like their Caucasian counterparts? You'd probably have sistas standing outside the barber shop with picket signs pleading for the brothas to "come on back home."

"You got some pretty hair girl ... "

Physical features such as skin color, hair texture, light eyes and hourglass figures determine to a great extent how women are treated in society. These days even some of our finest sisters will go to just about any length to erase what God has blessed them with. Whether it's fake hair, breasts, eyelashes, liposuction, or lip injections, many women (of all colors) will do just about anything to make their natural attributes disappear. S**t, some of your husbands have never even seen your *real hair*! In most cases, the imaginary flaws you see when you look in the mirror are all in your head. But that doesn't stop you from doing everything you can to change your appearance to fit whatever standard of beauty is the flavor of the month. There is enormous pressure for women to fit the mold of what they see every day on the magazine racks and television screens. Throughout the Black community especially, from kindergarten up little girls realize how important the texture of their hair is not only to their popularity in school but society as a whole. But along the way they'll also have to deal with the lifelong burden of "Oh she must think she cute."

NEWS FLASH!

Beige is beautiful too! And mixed babies get more attention. It's true. I went to the mall for my research. There I saw proud new Mommies and Daddies pushing their pride and joys from the toy store to the Food Court and everywhere in between. Today there are more interracial marriages and relationships which produce children than ever before in this country. But what really goes through that child's mind when she is called "Oreo" or forced to check "other" when asked to provide her race/nationality? Of course we all know that "jungle fever" was not always as accepted as it is now. During slavery, the number of interracial encounters reached its height, obviously due to the master/slave sexual liaisons that were commonplace at the time. After the Civil War, the numbers dropped, but since the sixties have continued to rise up till the present. These days you see interracial couples of all shades, ages and backgrounds walking hand in hand and living harmoniously. The truly intriguing part of this phenomenon lies in the dynamics. Dig this; it is more common seeing a Black male/white female couple than the other way around. I've always been curious as to why this is so. And to tell you the truth, I do feel a certain uneasiness whenever I see a Black woman with a Caucasian man. Least I'm honest. I guess it's just not that easy for me to forgive or forget. Be that as it may, attitudes are changing when it comes to interracial dating and marriages in this country. I guess in a perfect world color should not have so much say in the way we treat each other but we all know it does. There are cultural, genetic, physical, and emotional differences that must be considered. I mean, if I go to see *Amistad* with Sarah, after we leave the theatre the conversation is not going to be the same as if I went with Tanisha. For real folks! I mean, I really do wish that "Ebony and Ivory" could live in perfect harmony. Some would say they can (and do) already. Still I wonder how America will look twenty-five years from now as the trend of interracial unions continues to expand.

"Light meat or dark meat?"

There are many things we don't talk about. And it's indeed true that some things are better left unsaid. For instance, most white women have a Black man. I know that this may seem a bit hard for some of you to swallow but it's real. What I mean is that even though "Becky" may be happily married and otherwise stable and content, she either has a Black man she secretly lusts for or is curious about but chooses not to act on her impulse. In many cases however she *is* actually involved with him to some degree. As I said, I'm quite sure this has many of you uncomfortable, but this is part of the veil that covers our society as attitudes, lifestyles and stereotypes continue to change. I want a woman that is like my Mama. My sister wants a man that is like her Daddy. But sometimes she ends up involved with a man who looks like the cat that enters her dreams while she is asleep. It has always been interesting to me how light is attracted to dark and vice versa in today's society. Matter of fact I know more than one Caucasian female who dates Black men exclusively. As you may or may not know, the whole light-skinned, dark-skinned debate has a long and distinguished history in America. We could go into the whole "house n***a, "field n***a" thing but by now we all know the dynamics. But it's a subject that is usually reserved for "after hours" conversations or poetry slams than in prime time. Anyway, if Becky indeed does have a secret infatuation with Tyrone then the opposite must also be true due to the laws of physics and attraction. Yep. "Jack" has got a thing for "Tasha" as well. But of course this goes without saying. And it's easy to see why. But let's check out the flip side. These days it's commonplace to see an Amerfrican brother strolling by the pier with a white sister on his arm. But we all know this wasn't always the case. In fact there was a time when you'd find a brotha at the bottom of a river for simply whistling at a woman. Boy, how things have changed. It is what it is folks. So these days we barely even take a second glance when we see these combinations all over the place unless of course you happen to be in a place where it is not as accepted as it is here in the States. So in some ways we have become more accepting of certain dynamics and less tolerant when it comes to others. The construct of race we have come to embrace is slowly becoming obsolete. So yes, in a perfect world there is only one race, and that is the human race. But since most of us fall well short of perfection, the golden rule only seems to apply on special occasions. The truth is, each and every last one of us has, and will continue to play the "race card" whenever it is in our best interest.

Bottom Line: The bottom line is; watch what the hell comes out your mouth people!!! But more importantly check out what's goin' on upstairs in your head that forms the basis for your behavior. In an ideal world race/color/creed should not have such an impact on the way we treat others and are treated ourselves. But in this world it does and I'm glad. We are all different and bring unique delicacies to the table. At the same time we have so much in common there really shouldn't be nearly as much separation as there is. So it becomes more about respecting each other than pointing fingers and hurling insults. And one more thing. You notice how every time something happens it's always "gonna spark a whole new dialogue on race!" I swear if I hear that one more time I think I'm gonna choke somebody! I mean, how much more damn dialogue do we need? Folks, by now we pretty much know what time it is don't ya think?

5

WHAT'S LOVE GOT TO DO WITH IT?

✦

(Entertainment)

Tell me y'all, is it possible to be "in love" with someone (thing) that doesn't actually exist? Sure it is. In fact we see it all the time on the big (and small) screen as well as in real life. We "fall" madly in love with the most absurd things this crazy world has to offer like cars, clothes, pets, people … What other reason would you treat your poodle to a more expensive spa than you would for yourself! At this very moment many of you are smitten with someone/thing you KNOW just ain't no damn good for you. And you knew it after the very first date! "But what if she's the one?" Or "But I love him!" Okay, I know you do. But still I must ask you; does LOVE *really* have anything to do with it? I'm sure Tina Turner could answer much better than I, but last I heard she was a long way from Nutbush, Tennessee if you dig what I'm sayin.' I'm sure you could probably find her in Europe somewhere though, undoubtedly in a much better place than her days with Ike. Poor Ike … Bet you the script would've read a little different comin' from his side of the fence. But that's beside the point. The image of the Black man in movies and television has changed very little since the 1970's and the "black exploitation" film era in which pimps, players, pushers, and private "dicks" with all the chicks were in every theatre. So much in fact that films such as *The Mack, Superfly, Shaft, Willie Dynamite, the Black Godfather* are now required viewing for aspiring thugs, gangstas, hustlas and playas of today's generation. After all, it's cool to be the pimp. Mythologized on the streets and immortalized on the big screen, this ruthless, cold-hearted and of course money hungry creature's sole motivation was (and is) the almighty dollar. Armed with a stable of women who "work" for him exclusively, this ladies man fancies himself as entrepreneur, father figure, lover and best friend all in one. He offers guidance, direction and protection, usually preying on impressionable young females looking for LOVE. He's not always Black, but this certainly is the image that has been drilled into our heads since back in the day and that has reemerged in popular culture and hip-hop in particular. Regardless, the "mack" is all business with no time (or use) for emotional attachment or feelings. His most valuable asset is his ability to "spit game," or make the woman believe it's in her best interest to be on his team. I've always been fascinated by how we continue to portray these characters and usual suspects on television and in the movies. I can understand fifty, sixty years ago when the opportunities were scarce for Blacks in film but I have no explanation for this new "coon" school and its many pupils. I'm also intrigued by how (after all we've come out of) we can continue to portray ourselves in this buffoonish manner. True, it may no longer be "Yassuh boss, here I comes, right away suh!" but you still see many of the same stereotypes and images all over the place. Look here folks, the first and only way to restore our tarnished image is to *control* it. As I mentioned, young Black men are hardly the only pimps in the "game" but you wouldn't know it by the picture you are shown. The effect a visual has on your mind and what it processes is profound. And in the twenty first century the only way we can reverse the many stereotypes we've embraced is to control the images. You know as well as I do that not all white women are "loose," just as you know that not all Jews are tight with a dollar. You know that. But stereotypes have a way of growing legs and traveling at warp speed (especially in today's electronic age). Pay attention to the commercials on T.V and you will see the way various ethnic groups are portrayed. If the car ad is marketing the sporty coupe as "hot and sexy" observe the model featured in the spot. Is she a "dirty blond," brunette, redhead, Black chic? And if the ad is for the happily married father of three taking his family to Disneyworld chances are his name won't be Hector.

JUST CHANGE THE CHANNEL!

Basically what stays on the screen is whatever draws in the most eye-balls. The controllers of images make sure of that. Indeed, love seems to have very little to do with what we watch every night on the boob tube. In fact it seems more of an afterthought than anything else. It's usually SEX, *SEX* and more S-E-X that is magnified on prime time, so much so that you'd think it was "normal" behavior to meet someone at the coffee shop and jump into the sack with them after an espresso, biscotti and some small talk. Everything on the television is designed to let you know you're not good enough. Or rather; "Here's what good enough looks like." Either that or; "And tonight ladies and gen-tlemen one lucky contestant will walk away with a million dollars?" Just not *you!* Then there's the "reality" show where a bunch of folks are stranded on some deserted island and whoever can survive the longest without losing their minds wins the cash. And don't forget about the one where they swap spouses. All I wanna know is are these the same folks talking about family values when election time comes back around? Television is a very powerful tool folks, especially in the minds of small children who are not yet mature enough to filter all the images being thrown at them. It's not at all how it used to be when you could sit around the living room with your kids and enjoy some laughs without having to worry about what they'd see when you got up to grab the popcorn from out the microwave.

So once again dear brothers and sisters I ask; "What does love got to do with it?" Apparently not much let Hollywood tell it. I must say though, I do enjoy taking in a good action/adventure flick every now and then. And I definitely dig comedies. I've noticed that the low-budget slasher films are making a comeback as of late as well but I usually pass (nightly news is enough for me). But occasionally I'll check out a good "love" story to smooth everything out. And it usually works, but it's rare that I get to see a flick with brothas and sistas of the darker shade engaged in fruitful, healthy and wholesome relationships. Usually it's the same old' story line where the "leading man" is a lowdown, shiftless cat with a boulder on his shoulder who can't keep his d**k in his pants. You know the one where the sister he's involved with has a bunch of girlfriends lettin' her know just how much of a "dog" he really is. "Girl, you know he's f****n' everything that moves!" I'm right. To this day Black relationships and love continue to be reduced and trivialized on T.V. as well as the silver screen. The problem is not that filmmakers and television producers (Black or white) are unaware of the existence of productive, positive unions in our community. Perhaps they're just lazy. Funding is usually the major obstacle faced by filmmakers. But this is no excuse either for compromising the content of a picture. As many unique viewpoints and stories we have to tell it's amazing how misunderstood and grossly stereotyped we still are when it comes to movies. You'd think every Black woman was a single mom trying to hunt down her dead-beat "baby daddy" for child support. And don't let me get started on the image of "Ty Ty" tryin' to "run game" on every unsuspecting female in sight. Of course he's lazy, unemployed and good for nothin' except donating sperm. Am I lyin?' But such is the strange portrayal of Black love throughout the airwaves. You have to understand there were not always Blacks in Hollywood. But there were Black films and filmmakers *outside* of Hollywood even when segregation was at its highest peak. Where are they now? They're still making movies that's where. And many of them do have inspiring themes and messages which place the Amerfrican in a positive light. But you may not find those films in your local Cinema Multiplex.

AND THE ENVELOPE PLEASE

Some people work all their lives to become icons, idols, leading men/ ladies and all the rest. To be loved, admired and respected by your audience is very important to most artists and creative people in general. So it's no surprise that the infamous red carpet is the one place they get a chance to shine. They usually arrive all dolled up, washed, waxed, buffed and polished, skin smoother than a baby's ass looking younger than the last time we saw them. Why we're so fascinated with the lifestyles of the rich and famous to begin with is beyond me. But that doesn't stop me from tuning in just like everybody else. For me, it's pretty much to see if the Black actor/actress is going to win the big award of the night. After that I switch the channel to see what else is on. What really trips me out though is how these people actually spend their whole lives trying to be famous. Then when their dreams come true they spend the rest of their lives trying to avoid the spotlight, shielding themselves from the cameras by wearing dark shades, scarves, and bandanas to hide from the paparazzi and all the glare. I guess sometimes you do get what you ask for. But beyond the stretch limo, velvet rope and VIP section I've never understood our obsession with these gaudy awards shows and long-winded acceptance speeches cut short by theme music. But that's just me. If some of these awards shows were held in the 'hood you'd hear all types of "Get yo ass off the stage already man!" Or "ENOUGH motherf****r!" And what's even creepier than those strange looking trophies they smooch, cling to and covet is the reverence they seem to hold for them. But then again I never quite understood why someone would want another person's autograph either. True artists know that the greatest award/ reward they can receive is the heart (respect) of their audience. But we've put these people on such a pedestal that it is not uncommon for a "star's" name to fetch up to thousands of dollars in some cases just for their "John Hancock." When the measure of success is the acquisition of toys, trinkets and things that shine, gleam and glisten, we start to believe the illusion is real. And since we're emotionally shut down in so many ways it becomes easier to understand. Furthermore we

(Black people) want to be loved and accepted just like everybody else. It just shouldn't take bringing home a gold statue for us to feel like we've finally made it to the top.

MUSIC

In every culture music is an essential part of life. For Amerfricans this is no different. In fact Black people throughout the world have always had a special relationship with music. Or should I say rhythm. Throw in a touch of blues and you've got yet another art form for the world to imitate. But despite the Black influence and fingerprint on every form of music you see out here there is still a sense of "Who cares" when it comes to our own acknowledgement of the brilliant men and women who have brought so much *"Love and Happiness"* to our everyday lives. It's more than just the song you sing in the car on your way to work in the morning. For the majority of Black folks, music has taken on a much deeper significance in our lives. From the days of the drum up until today's soul/r&b, gospel jazz, reggae and hip-hop, music has always been therapeutic for us. It not only helps us through the day but eases our pain in tough times and puts smiles on our faces when things are great. Self expression has always been one of the Amerfrican's greatest assets. One glance at the dance floor at your local club will tell you that. Yet go to any blues or jazz spot around and you will see predominantly Caucasian audiences. Why is this so? Why do they respect the art and musical lineage of our forefathers and ancestors so much more than we do? To the extent that they've made it their business to study, collect and even imitate the soul greats and legends of yesterday. Nowhere in society can you see Black folks doing the work and not getting the credit more than in the music industry. Even before Elvis paid off his songwriters with Cadillacs and kept the publishing to buy Graceland the earliest blues pioneers were tricked and schemed out of what was rightfully theirs. And guess how much cash "Graceland" generates today? You don't really want to know do you? So now just fifty years later you see all these white boys at the top of the charts talking about "I remember the first time I heard that Al Green!" "Changed my whole life!" "I knew right then and there this is what I wanted to do with myself!" But this is not to say there are no genuine music lovers and collectors of all shades who are not just "fly by night" fans or opportunists trying to cash in on the genius and soul of our musical treasures. Many have more vintage, rare, out of print or limited edition records of your favorite artist than you even knew existed and are very respectful and knowledgeable of the culture of Black music. And they have no problem letting you know that they pledge allegiance. And sincerely so. Sometimes I wish we still did …

The point is, Black people (especially Amerfricans) are incredibly passionate yet very conservative even when it comes to artistic expression although you wouldn't think it observing some of the outlandish behavior we display on a regular basis. But it's true. And we have good reason to be. We've been through enough to realize that at any given moment some s**t could hit the fan not because of a casual off-handed remark or racial slur but simply because we're BLACK. So it's rare that you'll see a cat walking down the street dressed in tight leather pants, knee high boots and a cowboy hat like Rick James yellin' "POWER TO THE PEOPLE!" even if that's just how he feels that day. And if you did you'd try to get out of his way as quickly as possible talkin' 'bout "He must be high or somethin." Perhaps it's *you* that's really trippin!' What I'm trying to say folks is that true SELF-EXPRESSION in the Black community is at an all time low. And a lot of Black music smells more like "brown" music if you dig what I'm sayin.' Truth is, we all have something to say but usually are just afraid to express it. And so we end up paying lip service to how F'd up the status quo is while we go to great lengths to embrace it.

But back to Tina. Better yet Ike. What the hell ever happened to Ike anyway? Last I heard he was happily remarried and still doin' his thing on the circuit. By the way, did you know that Ike Turner is responsible for what is universally acknowledged as the first rock n' roll song in music history? Probably not. Check it out sometime. But I'm sure if you ask the wrinkled rockers that now make a billion dollars a year from playing sold out stadiums they know what time it is. Now if I asked if you remember the beat down Ike put on Tina in that limo I bet you could run down the whole scene! And believe me brothers and sisters love ain't got a damn thing to do with that ...

Bottom Line: We all want basically the same things in life, love and acceptance being at the top of the list. It's just that sometimes we go looking for them in the strangest of places. As for the entertainment industry, it's not about ratings. Well, it may be for those pulling the strings behind the scenes but that only means there is a desperate need for some new blood on that front too. The real question is are you willing to challenge yourself and your peers to tell it like it really 'tis? Hell, you know as well as I do Black people are as honest, trustworthy, dependable, hardworking, reliable, caring, nurturing, patient, kind-hearted, affectionate, intelligent, gifted, thoughtful, sensitive, funny and downright brilliant as anybody else right? WELL DON'T YOU?? So it's like this brothers and sisters. If you wanna hear something better then MAKE something better! If you can't stand the images you see every day on movies and television then create your own. Period.

6

HIP-POP

So here's what happened to me the last time I flew the friendly skies. Figured I was all set with my Ipod, laptop, and cell/camera phone. Only thing I needed before takeoff was a few snacks and last minute reading materials. First stop was the terminal bar for a couple drinks to take the edge off, then on to the nearest bookstore/souvenir shop for a magazine or two. So I head over to the magazine rack and the first thing I see? The latest pouty-lipped "it girl" in a two piece staring seductively in my face begging me to look at her sexy photo spread. Hard to tell if she's naughty, nice, attractive or anorexic. After a couple minutes the cute girl at the counter approaches: "Need any help sir?" "No thanks, I'm just looking" as my eyes roam to the next rack of HOT! SIZZLING!! STEAMY!!! new looks of the season. I scratch my head and make my way to the far left hand corner of the rack where a couple hip-hoppish looking magazines that make up the Black section rest. You've probably seen this section. It's kinda like the Alternative section of your local record store. Short and to the point. So I pick up the magazine closest to me and casually flip through it as I wait for my flight. Curious as to what my younger brothers and sisters are currently into, I make my way to a feature on 'Lil "So and So," the hot new rapper everybody's talkin' about this month. He's posing (like all the rappers pose), flashin' his gold "fronts" (teeth) all over the place like he just stepped off the video shoot. Crazy kids … only there's one slight difference between him and the rest of the "pimps," "gangstas," "thugs," and "killas" profiled in the magazine. He's white! That's right. And not just Caucasian, but European I believe. So I continue to flip through the article and read how this English rapper is doin' it for *"all my n***as in the hood,"* and I start thinking to myself "WHAT THE??? Before too long I set the magazine down, look in both directions and it finally dawns on me; "This thing is really outta control!" At this point everything starts to get a little hazy (probably the liquor takin' effect). Either way it's time for me to board my flight so I quickly snap out of it and head toward the departure gate. But before I do I take one last glance at "MC Henry" and say to myself "Are you kiddin' me?" You gotta understand, it hasn't always been like this. I came up in a different era folks. And I clearly remember when the absolute *last* face in the world you'd pull up to at the stoplight and see bangin' some hip-hop music from the back of the trunk would be of the Caucasian persuasion!

A lot of you out there know what I'm talkin' about. But regardless, today nowhere can you see the F.O.A.B.P at work than in the world of HIP-POP. Not to be confused with the hip-hop that I and many of you grew up and are familiar with. No my friends, this hip-pop is a whole new breed. All you have to do is walk down the street. Any street. Watch the youth. Check out how they're dressed, the way they carry themselves, walk, talk. The baggy jeans, oversized t-shirts, baseball caps and "do rags." And most importantly the ATTITUDE. If you feel brave enough, say something to these hip-poppers. Speak to them. They'd probably welcome the conversation. See, this is the problem. You older folks don't even talk to the kids anymore. But you sure do talk *about* them don't you? Yes you do. But when you were their age didn't you have grownups keeping an eye on you and making sure you were going the right way? Of course you did. So look here, it's the same beat these kids are boppin' to these days, just a different approach. You'd be surprised. These youth really do have something to say, if only you'd LISTEN!!! And don't be misled by the media either. They're not all rapping about flippin' birds, (hustling coke) pimpin' hoes and bustin' their Glocks (although that is part of the landscape too). But no more than you can say that all heavy metal rockers glorify Satan in their lyrics (although some do). There are scores of "conscious rappers" out there but they are usually relegated to "underground" status. I wonder why? It's because these tales of oppression have become a multi-billion dollar a year industry that's why! And I do mean BLACK OPPRESSION. The bottom line of course is the almighty dollar. And since the glorification of street life, crime, crack selling and N's and B's has somehow become the choice of this new generation we as well as the elders in our communities have no other choice but to accept what's being fed our younger brothers and sisters right? After all, kids will be kids ain't that right? Are you crazy? We all need to check ourselves. 'Cause if this keeps on going on as it is pretty soon we're all gonna get checked.

So here we are. And as many of you have heard by now, hip-hop is dead. Or at least in the E.R. But hip-*pop* continues to make the industry executives you never, ever see filthy rich times ten. Like any other art form there are changes and mutations involved, making way for this new form the kids are two-steppin' and finger-snappin' to. There's only a vague resemblance to the beat-boxin,' pop-lockin,' "boom bap" original rap which nurtured my classmates and I so many years ago. But who cares? Like I said, things change. And what the kids are talking about these days only reflects what they're absorbing from US! I mean, think about it. Young people, like the rest of us are products of their environment. And the truth is, rappers come from primarily disadvantaged circumstances and are willing to say just about anything to make it out of the "hood" right? Wrong!!! These days you have kids from all walks of life jumping into the game trying to "get that paper dog!" That's just how it is, like it or not. I must admit I could've never imagined the incredible impact this expression would have on not only America but the world. So much so that you have cats from every continent on Earth emulating their Amerfrican brothers' and sisters' style and grace. So let's take a closer look at the current status of this hip-pop and the shape of things to come.

HIP

Also known as "with it," "together," "down," sexy … being hip has always been synonymous with Black culture. And like it or not hip-pop follows in the great tradition of the many musical forms we have blessed the world with throughout history. It's also now the official voice of a new generation. And with it you get both the best (and worst) of our nature as a people. In the Jazz era of the forties and fifties, hip meant looking "clean," having style and most importantly being ORIGINAL. But even then the finest "threads," slickest hair and shiniest shoes couldn't replace the mastery and technical proficiency of the artist and his mastery over his particular instrument. We used to beat the drum. Today we beat the pads of drum machines and synthesizers. It's not the same thing. And this has become part of hip-pop's (and hip-hop's) Achilles heel. You see, in order for any art form to be successful and thrive over the long haul it must EVOLVE. Hip-hop for the most part was based on the use of two turntables, a microphone, mixer, assorted "beat" machines and musical samples. The culture also included graffiti art, break dancing, and street fashion. But you can only flip a beat so many ways before it becomes homogenized. After awhile it just all starts to sound the same. So unlike the blues, jazz, and rock n roll before it, hip-pop hasn't been able to evolve musically the same as the other forms which utilize live instrumentation. Be that as it may it has provided so many of our young brothers and sisters a way out of the ghetto, "joint," block hood *and* 'burbs and into a higher tax bracket and standard of living. And its influence cannot be denied. Today the word hip is synonymous with "fly," "fresh," "clean," "crunk" and the like. And so much money is changing hands that some of your favorite hip-pop stars' hotel suites are bigger than your house. But hip pop seems to have reached it's material peak. Ironically the only thing left to pimp has become … you guessed it, OURSELVES. And from the looks of things we're doing a mighty fine job of that thank you very much.

But what does this say for the generations to come? I mean, what does the future hold for the offspring of bling bling and the hustlers and playas that supply the streets with "that heat" that makes the guys get "buck" and the girls "drop it like it's hot?" Will the next generation of hip-poppers continue to ridiculously flaunt their "riches and b***hes" just as their Mamas and Daddies did? Or will they finally see the light and learn from the tribulations of their elders? Who knows? Maybe they'll choose to honor and respect their craft (and each other) and take the art form to a whole new level. Or maybe they'll continue to sell themselves short to the highest bidder for a mere fifteen minutes of fame and some conflict diamonds. Only time will tell. One thing's for sure. Hip-pop is now raising our children. It is also creating jobs for Black people. So it would be foolish for us to turn our backs on this one folks. There is no denying the power and influence of hip-pop across the land. That is, once you get past the tough talk, macho buffoonery, "ice grills" and flashy whips. The pulsating rhythm, hypnotic hi-hat, kick, snare and lyrics of the music can be heard everywhere from television commercials and feature films to weddings and sporting events. Presidential candidates now openly (or should I say cautiously) court the hip-pop generation's vote when just twenty five years ago it was casually written off as the new disco. But sadly enough, it is quite predictable how hip-pop has now ended up in the conference rooms and editing floors of corporations foaming at the mouth for another cash crop. (i.e. sugar, cotton) The new millennium rapper is a walking billboard, marketing everything from energy drinks and liquor to Hollywood movies. The positive aspect of hip-pop and its awesome potential lies in the fact that it has and continues to stimulate and grow entrepreneurs and businesses within the Black community. The amount of money that is being made by rappers from ventures such as clothing and fashion only underscores it's power and potential to effect change in the Amerfrican community. The flip side is this minstrelsy that has now infiltrated the industry, with "I GOT THIS AND YOU DON'T" as the new motto. Along with some of the questionable lyrics and demeaning portrayal of women there are many things to be concerned about within the hip-pop "game." There is a new found obsession of belittling one another for personal gain and "street cred" that is both fascinating and disheartening. And this is the problem. Just because the beat is hot (hypnotic) doesn't mean it has any lasting value. As Black people we are the most rhythm oriented people on the planet. And so we tow the line between what feels good to us and what may or may not be good *for* us.

THE GHETTO MASK

Here's what's so not hip. Everyone knows that looking rich doesn't mean you actually "got it like that." It just creates a situation in which you are forced to live up to an image that costs an arm and a leg to maintain. But many of our youth don't realize there are many other ways to be a baller/shot caller besides spittin' over a "hot track." It is up to us to provide them with more options. Rappers have a million aliases, a trillion nicknames and "skullies" and "hoodies" where crowns used to be. Two or three MC's use their born name, but this is rare in the hip pop game. Bottom line, rappers are AFRAID to be themselves. So they become stereotypes, caricatures, and distorted representations of "hip" with all the accessories that go along with it. The problem is that somewhere down the line they realized they could make a pretty penny pretending, bragging and boasting of material riches and sexual exploits (real or imagined). These new hip-poppers have quite a different agenda than their older hip-hop brethren and sistren, which you can hear loud and clear every time you turn on your radio. In a nutshell the message is "Get money, get *mo'* money, and then spend it on any and every object that symbolizes success. Then you're officially a "G." But have you noticed that all the trappings of success we "bust a cap in that ass" and "break down them bricks" for are never in the price range of the average Mo (or Moesha) in the neighborhood? And this only breeds jealousy and envy amongst the kids coming up wanting to be ballers. Sound familiar? Have you noticed that for every hip-popper who does his best not to perpetuate the common stereotypes associated with the genre there are ten more who do their best to live up to them? And since there are no "rap police" to enforce the rules and lock up these perpetrators they are left to run rampant all over the place. It's easy to see why. We all love the rags to riches, ashy to classy, get shot up, do time and live to tell it soundtrack of your favorite rapper. This tale has been woven into the impressionable young minds of the youth from the time their parents let them listen to these cats. Hip pop is the only musical form where the more criminal offenses you have, the more credibility you garner. No wonder they call a police record a "rap sheet!" I grew up in the era where the Parental Guidance/Explicit Lyrics logo first appeared on compact discs. This was in the late eighties/early nineties, when "gangsta rap" first gained mainstream notoriety and increasing acceptance. But this was before the "bling bling" era began. These days it doesn't pay to be conscious and in the hip-pop game. That's because the powers that have a strangle hold on these "coonish" images have a predetermined agenda. And it's quite obvious what they want our children to worship. Don't get it twisted my friends, Black people have always been "fly," And there have always been "playas," and hustlers in the Black community as there are in every other community in America. But due to our unique past and ongoing struggle for equality in this country, we suffer from an insecurity that dogs us no matter how much "paper" we get. The eighties' crack cocaine explosion in our major cities had a tremendous effect not only on the economy of the United States but also on the pockets of our youth who have always felt disenfranchised by the system. Almost overnight you began to see "Beamers," Benzes, Audis and Jettas with tinted windows, rims, and spoiler kits all over the place. Young Black men were making more money during the Reagan era than in any other period in American history. And this was reflected in the music. Yet for every hustla that actually made it out the 'hood there were dozens more that either ended up dead or in prison. And so by the time the crack game did eventually cool off in the nineties and towards the turn of the century, you started to hear the tales of ex-dope dealers glorifying the "good ole days" when they had the "block on lock" and the dollars flowed like champagne at a wedding reception. And since the youth of today are out of touch with hip-hop's origins, foundation and forefathers they are left with little direction other than "F**k the world, I gotta get mine yo!"

INDUSTRY RULE # 4090

Once again, record company executives don't give a damn about your talent, only how much revenue you can generate. You do this by a) having the "right look/story" b) creating a significant street "buzz" or c) a combination of a and b. You'd be surprised to find out how many of your favorite rappers ended up being tax-write-offs (casualties) of the system. But business is business, and Black people have not yet learned that no matter how loud you can make the crowd yell "Ho" if you ain't makin' the man no "dough" then you gots to go! Point blank. And there's always another playa waiting in the wings to take your spot. Believe that. Too often though we find ourselves infatuated with the shining lights of the stage, failing to realize that there are many positions within the industry that need to be filled. Not everybody is cut out for the hectic lifestyle and industry politics of the recording artist. Get in where you fit in! And who knows, maybe then you'll have the longevity of the execs that sign those fat checks. Real talk. Truth is, the average rapper's lifespan is less than that of an NFL running back. So by the time you even get to pop a 'lil champagne off the success of your first single, they've already got five more of you. Who needs that pressure? Meanwhile, the real "boss" is laughing all the way to the bank while you "rep your hood." Huh? It's time we got hip to the game people and stop signing our lives on the dotted line. Always read THE FINE PRINT brothers and sistas! The writing's been on the wall.

SLEEPING BEAUTY

It's hard out here for a pimp y'all. But it's even harder out here for a ho. It's true. Though demeaning women seems to sell hand over foot these days it's really gotten out of control. Truth is we're all hypocrites. And that's why we bob our heads to the beat while reciting every destructive lyric on one hand then on the other act like it's so disrespectful and offensive for our kids to listen to the stuff. We want it both ways. And you know why? Because most of us can relate to what these rappers are talkin' about (at least to *some* degree). In fact most of you have called a woman a B or H more than once! Still it's WRONG! We all know that.

And our sisters deserve better. But the youth have no way to filter the steady stream of images that keep being flooded into their headphones and on the television screen. Meanwhile we just look the other way. Then we act surprised when our young women suffer from identity issues and low self-esteem. But women weren't always portrayed like this in rap music. During the late eighties and early nineties there were several female MC's who clearly represented strong empowered sisters with much more to offer the world than a big butt and a smile. And they were respected by the fellas too. But as time went on their voices predictably were silenced to a mere whisper. Thus, many women now believe it's normal to walk around each day feeling less than the beautiful Black sisters they've always been. And they demonstrate this by portraying promiscuous "chicken heads" and video vixens with even less than half a brain. You see them three-quarters naked in videos gyrating and grinding for the camera, believing somehow that this will lead to bigger and brighter opportunities down the line. Sadly enough however, some of our most elegant and intelligent princesses have adopted the identical mannerisms of the same b***hes and hoes they swear up and down they're not! And this is where the F.O.A.B.P takes one of the most destructive turns of all. You see, as the sisters continue to internalize the repeated onslaught from these misogynistic MC's they also begin to question the integrity and intentions of the rest of the brothers out here. As a result we are seeing the dramatic increase of formerly heterosexual females "becoming" lesbians in order to reclaim their lost/stolen dignity. Folks, this is madness! And we must put a stop to it. IMMEDIATELY! Since the beginning of time our women have been by our side through thick and thin. They have nurtured our children, they have kept us sane. They have lifted our spirits and made us whole. So, a word to all my beloved sisters out there (of any shade): We do need you. We do appreciate you for standing by us when nobody else would. Do not, I repeat DO NOT listen to what these misguided brothers say about you. Show them who you *really* are ...

CODE OF THE STREETS

"Stop snitchin." "Trust no one." "Keep it real." These are just a few of hip-pop's most revered commandments. See, in hip-pop, everything becomes "THE STREETS." Ah yes, the infamous streets. They have the final say on whether a rapper is kissed or dissed. Go to the mall you see the streets. Catch a flick starring young Amerfricans and you can best believe you'll get more of the streets. You could even drive out to the corn fields of Kansas and hear the streets pumpin' from the speakers of a beat-up old Ford pick-up. The streets are now the young Black national anthem, fight song, and flag. Oh, and the club too ... These days the youth are wearing the streets with more pride than ever before. You hear "On my block and "In my hood" so often in rap songs it sounds like a damn broken record. IT IS!!! Lights get cut off, it's the streets, sell dope to your cousin, streets is cold. "Ain't no love in them streets baby." Just struggle, single moms and "baby daddies." Oh, and more street tales. So now you have thirty five year old grown men trying to speak the language of fifteen and sixteen year olds simply to honor the same streets they move out of as soon as their money gets right. This is dangerous y'all. We are stunting the growth of some of our sharpest and brightest minds by dumbing them down in exchange for 26 inch rims. In fact it's the same code of the streets that continues to have our most talented brothers shot down in cold blood and the tragic victims of yet another unsolved murder. Do they do this in country and western music?

POP

So now that we know what hip is, let's see what pop has to offer. Back in the day, those that ran the music business at least recognized and had respect for the role creativity played in an artist's development and evolution. Any highly creative person will tell you the best thing about being an artist is freedom. Usually they'll also tell you that if they weren't involved in their particular art form they don't know where they'd be or what they'd be doing. Pop, or popular music is very rigid in it's form and presentation. In other words, "If it ain't broke, don't fix it." The formula for what makes a "hit record" is tried and true. So the controllers of images are strictly in the business of finding "faces" that fit the shape and mold of whatever happens to be hot at the time. Remember the New Kids on the Block? Whoever's atop the charts you're likely to hear "Get me two more of those groups!" "I don't care where you find 'em, I just need two more of those!" As I said earlier talent is secondary to whoever can ship the most units and actually deliver in sales, 'cause everybody knows if it don't sell you get dropped like yesterday's newspaper. And depending on your "deal," you just might be able to make it out the door with your shirt on! Pop music is like fast food. Quick, painless, and with little to no nutritional value. It's good for bobbing your head as you ride down the street or "two steppin" at the club but that's about it. Other than that I can't call it. All Black music has a common thread. SOUL. Pop music on the other hand seems to lack this very element. The distressing part of hip-pop is that with all the negative images and stereotypes we continue to perpetuate it's getting harder and harder to recognize much less channel this soul effectively enough to rise higher. Shuckin' and jivin,' skinnin' and grinnin' reminds me of the minstrel shows of the past. The kids nowadays can recite every last lyric to "the latest jam" but can barely even spell S-H-A-C-K-L-E-S! And I'm not hatin' either. Just keepin' it real. Like I said, I come from the root and foundation of hip-hop (hip-pop's estranged Daddy). If anything I'm pulling for you young hip-hoppers to get your act together. But I also understand that the odds are heavily stacked against you. I mean, if all you're hearing in steady rotation is "Girl, wait till you see my d**k," then what the hell do you expect! And yes parents, this is an actual song! And it flew to the top of the *pop* charts! But no my friends, at the end of the day the kids are only partly to blame. Music reflects the nature of the times we live in. And the strength (or lack thereof) of the community. And today's times are recessive, watered down, derivative, and thoroughly unoriginal. During the 60's and the Motown era there seemed to be such an awareness and genuine concern about what was going on in the world, and the songs bore witness to this. There were songs protesting the Vietnam War, songs dealing with racial injustice, and songs dealing with genuine human emotions and current events. And these songs were sung by the youth of that time! Where are those songs today? If it ain't "I wanna lick you all over baby" then it's "Bend over girl show me what you workin' with!" Back then when you threw your hands in the air, the last thing on your mind was wavin' 'em like you just didn't care. There was too much to care about!!! But once again that was then. And yesterday's consciousness has been replaced by "If you don't give a damn we don't give a f#@k!" Are you kiddin' me? Many of you hip-poppers swear your s**t don't stink. Yet on every song you keep tryin' to put deodorant on that "funk" you call music. So you might as well stop. As you see my beloved brothers and sisters there's more than enough finger pointing to go around when it comes to this hip-pop. For now though just remember that you hold the key to your future. It's all up to you. You can either rise to the challenge and show the world what you're really "workin' with" or get steamrolled by the forces that already have pegged you as the obvious scapegoat to America's woes. So finally:

A MESSAGE TO ALL HIP-POPPERS

WAKE UP!!! You have been given a unique opportunity to have your voice heard by millions and millions of people the world over. Do not ever take this for granted. Be clear about your intentions, your music, and most importantly your mission. And remember, a lot of folks gave their lives just so you can have the opportunity to let the world know how you *really* feel. And that's what's up …

Bottom Line: Things changed after Tupac and Biggie got shot. Their unsolved murders took much more of a toll on our subconscious than we even realize. Understandably it only confirmed our worst fears and fueled so much misguided violence directed at our own that now every other MC is prepared to "kill every n***a in sight." But everything happens for a reason people. And this may be your final call. Thus my message to all young hip-hop/hip-poppers out there is this: First and foremost, BE YOURSELF!!! It's okay my young brothers and sisters, it really is. The universe will accept you whether you go platinum or wood. And chances are you will feel better about yourself if you start really "keepin' it real." WE NEED YOU, your passion, energy and most importantly your VOICE, not some perverted distortion of what you think we want to hear. Stop selling yourself (and us) short. Take your mind from the 'hood to the next phase of life and recognize your value to the children that are coming up after you. The creativity you possess is awesome but it also carries an enormous responsibility. Always consider your INTENTION even before you decide to pick up the mic. Oh, and one more thing; respect the sisters will you? They deserve more than what you're giving them. Look here, we all know there are females whose behavior leaves much to be desired and even may fit the description of B or H. But the truth is, all the name calling and degradation will only weaken YOU in the long run. So promise me you'll cut it out okay? At least try! We love you. PEACE!

P.S: Special shout out to Chuck D and Public Enemy.

7

WE DON'T ALL WANT BMW'S

"What do we want?"

F-R-E-E-D-O-M!

"When do we want it?"

NOW???

Really? In America class is rarely discussed openly. It's more or less taken for granted that your boss has a higher standard of living than you based on the simple fact that, well he's your boss. We generally look down upon those we consider "lower class" and envy/ogle the "upper crust" of society, white or Black. But the class struggle is taken to new dimensions when it comes to how we relate to each other. So you have poor Blacks snickering under their breath; "Bougie ass muhfu**as need to take they ass on back to the suburbs!" "Y'all worse than the g**damn crackas!!" Conversely you have your more "well-to-do" Blacks talking about "What they really need to do is quit complainin." "It's simple, get your ass off the couch and get a J-O-B like everybody else!" Most of you fall into one of these two categories. But my question is; how does this name calling help our growth and development as a people? Exactly, it doesn't. So why do we continue to engage in this nonsense? Because many of us suffer from the "If I did it anybody can do it" syndrome and instead of truly listening to each another we constantly prejudge and label one another making it damn near impossible to reach any type of understanding. In reality though, this whole class discussion goes beyond Black or white and into the "green" zone. All you have to do is go to the hills of Appalachia or the trailer parks of Ohio and you'll see as many wiggas (white n***as) as you will Black n***as on the streets of Brooklyn, Harlem, or the South side of Chicago. By now we're so busy trying to keep up with the "Jones's" that we literally have no time to even consider creating opportunities for others. "Man last thing on my mind is some damn revolution bull***t." Or it's "Ni**a I got kids!" So did Malcolm. 'Member him? … Either way, none of us wants to admit that we still carry the chains of slavery, mentally so now more than ever. But we're eternal optimists. So now you see the increase of Black Republicans springing up all over the place talking about family values and such as a last gasp attempt at trying to fit in. Black people are neither Democrat nor Republican! So really it all comes back to our individual perception of success. Just because you receive a paycheck doesn't mean you are FREE. Sorry. It doesn't work like that in America. All we are doing at this point is pumping it back into the system as soon as we get it anyway ain't that right? And at the end of the day in America you either fall into one of two categories: the HAVES and the HAVE-NOTS.

THE HAVES

So like I said, Black folks have a strange perception of success and what it looks like. The outer appearance of those who've risen to the top tier of corporate "success" tends to be on the conservative side, as does the social and political outlook of the so-called middle class. Since "making it" involves mixing and mingling with all different types of people it is not uncommon to see older Black men in button up dress shirts, pin stripe suits and bowties (wing tips are optional).

After all, it is important to dress for success. But as our suits get tighter and teeth whiter there seems to be a disconnect which separates the haves from the have nots. For one, the haves are able to travel. Meaning they have the financial flexibility to get on a plane at anytime and go any place they choose. This is significant seeing as how many people, Black or white have never even seen a passport, much less used one to travel outside their particular neighborhood. Another thing I've noticed is the haves seem to get paid whether they're at work, the golf course or sipping Mai Thais thousands of miles away from home. Their money seems to work for them and not the other way around. They also tend to be owners/employers rather than employees which allows them this unique flexibility. Unfortunately amidst the hustle and bustle of the forty hour work week this concept of ownership is one which we've had a tough time grasping. Therefore the rat race has become our chosen means of realizing the American Dream. Fortunately there are different classes of race rats. 1)There are those who work downtown and commute/carpool to the office. 2)There are those who drive themselves to work and park in the garage. 3)Then there are those who work at the mall and park in the parking lot. 4)And finally those who have a driver who opens and closes the door behind them and could care less where he parks! Where do you fit in?

THE HAVE NOTS

The have-nots fall into quite a different category (and tax bracket) than their more affluent associates. They often work for minimum wage (if that), live paycheck to paycheck and have to deal with monthly rent as opposed to a mortgage. The disadvantage of this of course is that at the end of their lease agreement they either must extend this arrangement for another period of time yet build no equity (financial stake) towards eventual ownership. A great deal of the American Dream has to do with home ownership. And this is the dilemma many in the Amerfrican community (especially in urban areas) are faced with. They are basically giving their money away for room and board. But if you can't afford to buy a house for whatever reason what other option do you really have? Exactly. So the have-nots enjoy a different standard of living and are faced with a whole host of separate challenges than the haves. Challenges such as added "stress," poor diet, high blood pressure, and the overall struggle of reaching for "higher" things. In this shadow world you see folks working in "unskilled" positions for longer hours and less pay than their have counterparts. Then there are the homeless. The homeless remain the invisible face of America and are largely ignored and not even considered in the census (population count). These "poor white trash," "ghetto dwellers," and victims of unfortunate circumstances are somehow considered less human than those who have attained a certain level of financial independence and security. They come in all shapes, sizes and colors to be sure and you give them spare change and "God Bless" whenever you can. It's hard to see Amerfrican brothers and sisters living like this but for the have-nots this predicament is often just a couple paychecks away. So even though we no longer are "the village" we once were we still have brothers and sisters all over the place living in villages, tents, and underneath the overpass (as well as the YMCA).

Predictably money has become many people's (Black or white) spouse. They go to sleep at night with it on their minds and wake up in the morning with plots and schemes on how to get more. Back in the day cats kept their stash underneath the mattress or their "secret" spot for safekeeping. Today folks are damn near bathing in them "dead presidents." It's just the way it is. Money is the root of all evils. But it can at least afford you a few more options like getting away for a month or two each year. This is the ultimate paradox. When your pockets are bulging you feel more energized, confident and less stressed than when you only have three dollars to put in the gas tank, especially when gas is nearing $4.00 a gallon in some places. In other words, money makes you feel better about yourself when you have a lot of it and downright depressed when all you're coming up with is lint. That's why if you're unemployed you're better off keeping it to yourself. Nobody wants to hear about it. All they wanna hear is "Yeah man, everything's great!" In reality though, if you're one of the millions of folks dealing with money worries of any sort chances are life ain't as groovy as it would be if you could click your heels and hit the Lotto.

"So what do you do?"

Deal with it. Here we live to work as opposed to the other way around. Sit in a bar in another country, strike up a friendly conversation with someone and chances are the first question that comes out *won't* be "So, what do you do?" Granted, it may be the third or fourth but probably not the first. Conversely, hit your local watering hole down the road here in the States and you may not have time to get your name out before the question is asked. This is because of the way class is perceived in America. Here your identity, self-image, and appearance/attractiveness is closely related to what you do for a "living." You're not paid to think, you're paid to *do* in America. But consider this my friends; what makes one man worth $25/hr., another man $250/hr., and the next man $250,00 for two hrs? Could there be *that* much difference in their skill level? Please. Truth is, you've probably made a conscious choice to work for less than you are worth. And then you have the nerve to complain! Okay you're right there is no such thing as a noble occupation and the bills do have to get paid. But nobody forced you into that five hundred dollar car note either brotha! Truth is, some jobs just pay better than others, which gnaws at you so much that all you want to do when you get home is fix yourself a leftover turkey sandwich, have your old lady fetch you a cold one and kick back in your favorite chair. I'm right. Just recently I heard that a certain European soccer player from England had signed on to play in the States for an American franchise. They're paying him $250,000,000 for five years. That's right, TWO HUNDRED AND FIFTY MILLION DOLLARS for five years. Are you kiddin' me? That's like $6,000 an hour. What in the world could possibly make this man so special? Very simple, he has transformed himself into a commodity that is considered marketable or somehow more valuable in society than YOU HAVE. And you can best believe he's doing it outside the "box," or traditional forty hour framework we have so easily adopted as our own. Can you imagine Mike Tyson behind a desk selling life insurance? Back in the day it was not uncommon for an employee to stay with the same company for thirty, thirty five years. Today this is virtually unheard of. The average employee changes careers what, three, four times? (if not more) Furthermore, you'd be surprised how many folks have become jaded by the traditional nine to five/ten to six world and just decided to drop out altogether. Some by choice, others just because. Still, unemployment ain't what it used to be that's for sure. Not if you got bills to pay or mouths to feed. And it's not even limited to Amerfricans by any means. The work force is filled with folks of all shades who are more than willing to sacrifice their individuality in exchange for some "scratch." Let's face it, none of you really like your jobs anyway. Not *really* ... alright maybe a couple of you do but you're the exception rather than the rule. In most cases you just go because you have to which ends up leaving a sour taste in your mouth and a frown where a dream used to be. But whatever happened to the "REVOLUTION?" Remember that word? You know like when you see the documentary on PBS of the people carrying Marcus Garvey on their shoulders and thousands flooding the streets of Harlem just to hear him speak? I'm too young of course to have experienced it firsthand so I can only imagine the pride and sense of purpose this must have sparked in Black people at that time. Still it makes me think to myself; WHAT WAS ON OUR MINDS THEN? Sadly enough these days there's not enough time for revolution. Our schedules just don't permit it. On top of that we're still scared of that word considering the tragic fate that befell all the revolutionaries that came before us. Seems like they all either ended up in prison, "cracked out" or on the campaign trail minus their facial hair. You don't hear me though. So even if the revolution was circumci … I mean televised you'd probably just change the channel anyway.

As you know by now success in America also comes with its share of issues. As we work harder, get paid less and spend way MORE than anybody else we constantly put ourselves in financial jeopardy. Then we stress out after they cut off our cable for the fourth time in six months. Right now there are more homes up for auction at the courthouse due to foreclosure than ever before. But this is just another effect of trying to live beyond our means. Black people are in no way the only people who buy what we can't afford, but the difference is we still haven't fully grasped the importance of filtering our monies back into our own community. So how can we really expect to pull ourselves up from our own bootstraps/bra straps when as soon as we get paid we're up in the store buying "gators" and eight inch pumps? The haves do bear some responsibility in passing some of their wealth (or at least the knowledge of how they obtained it) to the future generations. But first they have to come down to Earth. The reality is that rich people tend to hang with other rich people and poor people … well they just feel the pain. And you don't even want to get me started on the middle class.

MS. THANG

Most women believe that it's a man's world, love it or leave it. They will also admit (when their defenses are down) that they have a burning desire to be on a level playing field with men and consider themselves as intelligent, if not more intelligent than their male counterparts. All the studies suggest that women are making humongous strides within the workplace in terms of income, advancement, and opportunity in relation to men, slowly but surely. Still a lot of Black men are less than ecstatic with the fact that their woman makes more than they do. "I got my *own* money, I don't need his money." This sentiment goes beyond racial lines, but the fact remains that the higher a Black woman climbs the corporate ladder, for whatever reason the more alienated she becomes from her Black brothers. It is also true that in many cases a woman has to be that much sharper than a man to reach the same level in corporate America. She's gotta be tough, yet not overbearing, ladylike, but not a pushover. Therefore she is forever walking that line, watching what she says and perhaps more importantly how she says it. You see it in the way she dresses for success, usually very reserved in her long pants and tailored business suits. In other words like a man. It's hard to imagine a time when women didn't work outside the home, but it's true. The Women's Liberation Movement of the 1970's had a lot to do with the entrance of women in the workplace, and today in many instances they are just as financially independent as men (if not more). The relationships between men and women in the office and all the dynamics that accompany it are very complex indeed. This is because the testosterone laden man will always view his female co-worker as a sexual opportunity/conquest (especially if she is attractive). It does not matter how business like she carries herself, it is the nature of the male to think sex. Which means you really gotta watch what you say around the water cooler, 'cause even uttering the wrong thing could land your ass in sensitivity training quicker than you can say "But I didn't mean it like *that!*" The irony is that many of the women I know who have stable, "professional" gigs seem to have A-1 credit as well which means a lot of us guys could learn a thing or two about money management from some of these sisters who've got their "thang" together. Don't get me wrong either, the number of upwardly mobile brothers in the workplace is also growing despite the unique challenges and obstacles he continues to face along the way, and this is a beautiful sight to see indeed. Now it's time to pool our resources together instead of always thinking it's a competition.

"It's taken me years to get where I am ... "

And that's why you believe that you're no longer a slave. In fact there are many of you who believe slavery ended. You probably read

this in a book somewhere or were taught it in childhood by misin-
formed schoolteachers. It was important that you got this (mis)infor-
mation at an early age, for even a casual glance at your current
surroundings would have told you otherwise. Only the slave can abol-
ish slavery. But first he's gotta want to stop, just like the alcoholic or
drug addict. Amidst the hustle and bustle, children to raise, things to
buy world we have created for ourselves it's very easy to get caught in
the matrix. They don't call it the rat race for nothin.' And the rats are?
As we enter the twenty-first century, the face of slavery has gotten the
ultimate "makeover." The gold package indeed; nose job, facelift,
botox, the total package … making it hard to see what's goin' on
beneath the surface. Yet most of us are closer to the poverty line than
we think. There are also a lot of highly intelligent brothers and sisters
on the street with families, friends, and bills too. You see my friends
the "real world" of nine to five functions as the perfect diversion to
finding self. It just affords you the opportunity to finance your particular standard of living and the toys that come along with it. But this
ends up leaving a sour taste in your mouths as you find yourselves
basically going through the motions and acquiring more "things."
These days the twenty-first century slave crosses all boundaries and
ethnicities. The brotha/sista is usually fairly "together" with a decent
amount of imagination/education, is racially aware to some degree
though not necessarily visible or active in her own community, financially motivated yet without any obvious sense of direction or mission. He shoots hoops every other week or so to stay in shape, tries to
eat right, drinks socially, smokes occasionally, may or may not be
married with children. In other words, she considers herself stable to a
large extent. Which means he's not willing to do or say anything to
jeopardize his position within the system, essentially leaving him with
no VOICE. See, no man in his right mind wants to cut his own
"nuts," especially the Black man who has said and done all the right
things to get to where he is. "Keep your mouth shut and hold onto
your job." And no self-sufficient, independent female wants to let her
sistas and herself down by rockin' the boat either. That is until her

number comes up or he hits the glass ceiling. Straight up. It is tragic though to see an upstanding citizen, Black or white give his blood, sweat, and tears to the company only to be disposed of like yesterday's news at the ripe old age of 57, without as much as a pot to piss in (much less health insurance). Guess who becomes a "burden" on the system then? See my friends, there is a huge difference between looking for a job and finding a reason (purpose) to work. And even if you do find yourself "comfortable" in your nine to five it is much easier than you think to make yourself one-dimensional. But just imagine what this country would look like if the twenty-first century slave would rise up and take his rightful place!

BRAINSTORMING

One day I'm gonna open my own business. I've been thinkin' either hair care products, a laundromat or car wash. Something that could provide a service/product to my people and at the same time put money in my pocket. I know my beautiful Black sisters can never have enough Pink Lotion or "no-lye relaxer" so that's a win-win situation off the top. And my brothers are gonna always stay clean regardless. So maybe I'll lower the price to seventy five cents a wash and the dryers to like … a quarter for double the minutes? I don't know. The car wash is a no-brainer for all y'all who like to ride around on them chrome "spinners." So now all I've got to deal with is how I'm gonna get some financing (start-up capital) to get the ball rolling. Guess first thing I need to do is get a copy of my credit report to see exactly where I stand huh? Then I'll take my business proposal to one of them Amerfrican banks and see if they can hook a brotha up with one of them low interest loans. Cross you fingers for me aiight? I'll let you know how it turns out. Anyway, as a youth I was taught (led to believe) that the highest professions were doctor and lawyer. Only thing they forgot to tell me was that doctors and lawyers have some of the highest rates of suicide around! Perhaps it's the pressure of having to repay the outrageous debt they incur just to be recognized in society as professionals. The trade-off however can be excruciating as now you see more and more of these high paid pros unable to cope with the pressure and turning to dope and the same medications they're prescribing to their "ill" patients!

"I went to college to ... "

Come to think of it, I'm not exactly sure why I went to college. Guess I just felt it was what people did after high school. At least in my family anyway. So I ended up at a HBCU (historically Black college/university) just like both my parents and sister before me. This turned out to be an invaluable and life-changing experience to say the least. For the first time in my life I went to school with, studied, played sports and partied strictly with people who looked, dressed and spoke like me. I also experienced a sense of pride that I had never felt before, and on top of that college sheltered me from the "real world." Some of the sharpest, brightest, and wealthiest minds in society can be found at these institutions, where sending children is just as much of a family tradition as Europeans and Ivy League schools. (not that either is mutually exclusive) Anyway it was in college that I got my first taste of freedom. Away from home, on my own and lovin' every minute of it. But I still had no clue what I was there *for*. I must've changed my major three, four times in my first couple years alone. But soon I began to notice what the game was all about. It was basically about processing information for short periods of time, usually just long enough to score well on quarterly exams, mid-terms, and finals. College wasn't really about critical thinking or even gaining knowledge or wisdom as much as it was about selective memorization and girl chasin.' In every one of my classes I felt like I was being taught not how to think, but what to think. And every spring, a couple months before graduation there would always be a mad scramble amongst the seniors about to enter the "work force." Recruiters from all the big corporations, firms and agencies would come to pluck the top students and offer them internships and jobs. I saw the pressure the students put on themselves to be what they believed these companies were looking for, changing their appearance, mannerisms and body language just to land a position with one of these prestigious companies. And seeing as how my grades were nowhere near the top of my class I had a chance to really observe (from a distance) how this wheel spun. By the time I became a junior, some four and a half years after I started, I began to ask myself if college was really for me. I started thinking to myself; "Education" must be more than a means of climbing the corporate ladder. But one lasting impression my college experience instilled in me was that we're taught to be employees. From the time we reach high school we learn this from watching our parents, older siblings and friends who have gotten their schooling and entered the work world exactly what we have to look forward to. We see it from all angles, and this leads us to believe the only way of taking care of ourselves is getting a job working for somebody else, saving a few bucks every paycheck, and if we have anything left over looking for opportunities to invest. This has become the definition of RESPONSIBILITY. But we are rarely, if ever encouraged, guided, and most importantly SHOWN how to be OWNERS for some reason. This slave mentality keeps us trapped in an imaginary box, unable to see that the only way to truly attain the dream is to own the team. Players change, get old and are eventually replaced by younger, fresher legs. Owners remain, protecting their investment, and raising ticket prices every other year knowing you'll gripe for a couple of days but will still pay the difference. That is, if you want to keep your season tickets. Free enterprise is the cornerstone of capitalism. But this is what our parents NEVER teach us. For some reason the idea (and practice) of generational wealth is still a mysteriously foreign concept within the Black community. It's as if many of our elders somehow think the youth will mystically obtain the knowledge of money management, financial planning, investment strategy etc … from thin air (or Mr. Trump). Meanwhile millions of Americans (and Amerfricans) don't even have a checking account! Once again this phenomena stems from our distorted image of success and the responsibility we've forsaken to the young ones we've brought into the world. Yet when they are infants we're quick to announce; "I swear my baby ain't gon' never have to go through what I done been through!" It could be as simple as a father starting a lawn cutting service for his son or showing him how to prepare taxes in order to teach him the basic principles of business and economy. Or a mother teaching her daughter how to sew and quilt, for when a child knows how to do SOMETHING it not only builds self esteem but character and business sense. Simple qualities like finishing a job, building something, and being proud of having your own can take you a long way in this world. After all, everybody knows that you'll work harder for yourself than you ever will for somebody else right? But since most of us are not bold enough to do what we love and EXPECT to be able to make a living from it, we end up punching the clock. Have you ever even thought about how this sounds? Punching a clock … almost like the clock is your enemy. Go to lunch, make sure you punch out now. Take your break, don't forget to punch out. But don't worry, if you do "forget" to give the clock a stiff right cross, best believe whoever's in charge of the whip (I mean) time sheet will surely take care of it for you.

"When I get money I'm gonna …"

At what point my friends do we refuse to be exploited? At what point do we refuse to exploit ourselves? As I said earlier, we don't trust each other to begin with. It's sad, but perhaps more true now than ever before. In this new millennium poker game it's all about "gettin' mine," and by any means necessary. We still fuss and fight over the pettiest of pettiness then wonder why collective prosperity is still a dream. And we certainly don't mind spending our hard earned dollars with every other ethnic group but our own. I ain't hatin' brotha, just statin' the facts that's all. You'd think we would have learned by now. There are always bright spots in the community but for the over-whelming majority of Amerfricans this basic principle is still often ignored when it comes time to put our money where our mouths are.

"It's my money, and I'll spend it however I damn well please! ... "

And that's your prerogative my brother. Completely. But is it all about you? Truth be told, you have probably become stagnant in your job anyway. And as time drags on you are becoming increasingly dissatisfied with the stagnation. Your HEART is just not in it. This is because you were taught that the only way to achieve "security" is to ignore your natural inclination (passion) and submit to a job with benefits. And now you've grown comfortable *and* complacent which makes it hard for you to muster the energy to actually follow your true calling. It's true. But it's not too late. In fact it's the perfect time, otherwise you wouldn't be thinking about it so much. Might as well go for it now because before you know it'll be Friday again and you'll find yourself scratching your temple wondering where the time went. I remember when I was eighteen and thirty seemed like a lifetime away. When I reached around twenty seven though, thirty didn't seem quite as far off, more like right around the corner. And when I hit thirty I was like "So *this* is how it goes!" Before you turn around it's Christmas again. Then New Year's, Easter, Thanksgiving and all the rest. These holidays have become our reference points for the passage of time and how we're using it. As the seasons change we find ourselves taking stock of where we are, where we've been and where we're headed. Old friends begin showing their age. Then when you look in the mirror it dawns on you that they're not the only ones! So whatever it is that you find yourself constantly debating whether to "go for it" or not let me assure you that you already know the answer to that one.

Remember how you used to talk about all the things you were gonna do once you "made it?" Had it all planned out too, down to the wood grain on the BMW, color schemes in the new crib and the grill on the deck. You probably never knew exactly how you'd get these things, but were always taught "Hard work pays off" and you believed it. You also probably were never told what it means to be

AVERAGE, though you may have only had to look around you to figure this out as well. Many of us have extreme personalities, and some choose not to subject ourselves to the nine to five, forty hr. work week. Others are just not cut out for it. This is not a negative. After all, at the end of the day most nine to fivers have way more clothes, "weed," and car money than bank money anyway! It's true. It's also true that most people will try to talk you out of your dreams, especially once you reach a certain age. But there will always be that one person who lets you know it's okay to trust your instincts and go for it. Listen to her. This may be the only way for us to make the road smoother for our sons, daughters, nieces and nephews. Follow your TRUE calling brothers and sisters and stop settling for a job that just pays the bills. For real. Otherwise there will always be shoulda, wouldas and couldas in your rear view mirror as you head to the office in the morning. You never know what can happen if you just try. But you do know you'll probably regret it if you don't. Chew on that for awhile.

Bottom Line: I'm looking for a different kind of freedom from now on. Or maybe just a different kind of feeling when I get up in the morning. Something that lets me know that I'm doing more than just bringing home the bacon. Hell, I don't even eat pork in the first place! Basically I want to feel like my job and my LIFE are linked by more than a paycheck and 401K plan. The satisfaction of knowing that I'm being true to myself and all the things that make me the unique individual that I've always been is as valuable to me as anything else. How 'bout you?

8

ADRENALINE!

Hi, I'm *Your Name Here*

And I'm a _____ a-holic.

Listen folks, we all know that drugs ain't no good. But neither is anything else you find yourself craving, whether it's triple cheeseburgers, Wild Turkey, Gucci or coochie. We all enjoy feeling high and feeling good from time to time. And most of us are able to handle our share of social drinking or occasional using without going too far over the edge. Take myself for instance. I drink cognac. I also drink water. I like them both. But I'd probably find it boring if I had to choose one and completely give up the other. They say the key is moderation. Sounds right. But whatever your wheelchair is, there's always a chance at some point it will become that crutch you always swore up and down it never would. "Aw man, never me! I just like to party once in a while that's all." "You know me, I can handle my liquor." Yeah we know. That's what they all say. But why exactly do people puff Kools and pop pills with funny looking names in the first place? Wanna know the truth? No apparent reason. Straight up. And although drugs do make you feel good (if only for a moment), it's really the anticipation of the high that keeps you going back for seconds, thirds and ... also why so many of our brightest and most talented Black, brown, white, red, even yellow brothers and sisters ultimately fall head over heels in love with them. With all life's ups and downs it's only natural for folks to seek some sort of relief from it all. And what better way to smooth things out than a cocktail or four? Once you get that first exposure to your craving of choice the next thought that comes to mind is *"Damn*, that shit was good!" Then it's off to the races, and inevitably goes from once a month to once a week, once a day to once an hour and so forth and so on. But when is enough ENOUGH? We all do have a different threshold or tolerance level for the weed, pills, blow, ice, E, glue … the list goes on and on and on some more. Pick your poison. It's everywhere these days and affect us all in one way or another. So if it isn't a family member or loved one battling a substance and the ups and downs this struggle brings it's a personal friend, acquaintance or co-worker. Truth be told, most of us have paid a visit to the offices of Dr. Feel Good at one point or another, although probably never to the point of running through the forest buck naked hugging trees … That's for the losers on COPS. For those of us who have dipped or dabbed before we know it's all about that RUSH! And even if you've never actually tried drugs yourself, you've probably played the role of enabler or encourager at one point or another. Adrenaline opens closed doors folks, sometimes ones you never even knew existed. And that's why they are so popular in all levels of society. Matter of fact your favorite musician probably used them to write all those cool songs you sing all the words to. But when it ends (and it ALWAYS does) you end up spending the rest of the night trying to recapture the feeling of that first (or last) time. Ninety percent of the time the cycle starts with alcohol. For myself, Olde English 800 was the dominant language in my neighborhood as a teenager growing up. My homeboys and I spoke it fluently too. The rush this liquid courage provided was second to none, that is if you could handle the next day's hangover. I remember so many nights of "blindness" off that potion I could barely move the next morning. But I had fun! The point is, we all want to feel good, and if it takes a couple tokes of the "chronic" to smooth that thang out a bit, so be it. But when it comes to the "hard stuff", we enter a whole new ballgame. And once you decide to enter the deep blue sea of "You wanna hit this?" it's really just a crap shoot.

ON ANY SIDE STREET

Things change when the sun goes down. "Hey! Hey, over here!!" "What you need man?" "Yeah, I got that." "Uh huh, yeah go 'head, pull up right over there." "How many you want man?" "Hurry up dude, it's hot out here!" "How many you want??" "Aiight, gimme your bread …" Street pharmacy is big business folks. The block is filled with small time dealers, "lookouts," and stick-up kids all trying to come up. There's a whole hierarchy in the hood (and burbs too). And they don't all wear baggy jeans and sneakers either. But they can get you whatever you need, from muscle relaxants to meth. Need to take a drug test? No problem. You can buy anonymous "piss" for five dollars if it comes down to that. But as usual it's a trade-off man. Living outside the system is tough. I mean, you could probably pay your rent and feed your seed if you have a strong enough "work" ethic, a few reliable clients, and the discipline it takes to save some bread. But you may have to jockey for position amongst all the other cats tryin' to get paid. These days hustlers are steadily finding new and improved means to move that product without getting their hands dirty. You even got cats doin' their business over the computer! Truth is, there's no such thing as easy money. But there definitely is such a thing as fast money. The problem many dope dealers face is that despite having walk-around cash and re-up money, they still don't OWN anything! It's not that they can't afford to purchase a piece of land somewhere or a luxury vehicle. It's just that for "legal" purposes it is wiser to put it in their girl, Mama, or auntie's name. The real question is why in the hell would a twenty year old kid risk his entire future for a fat knot, some fresh sneakers and a coupe in the first place? The answer? Because it's cool. Now don't misunderstand me, it's hardly cool to someone like you or I who knows better, but it surely is to a young kid who's only mentor/role model is the cat around the way with the flyest whip and the iciest chain.

LEGAL PUSHERS

We don't consider prescription pills *real* drugs, all we know is we're looking for a remedy for all this anxiety that's got our insides twisted up in coils and knots. Aerosol cans and glue sniffers excluded, we have become a society of pain-numbers willing to pop anything that dulls our senses. The truth is, these "medications" so readily prescribed by your physician are in many cases more addictive than the very street drugs you despise and turn your nose up at. But since you trust your doctor exclusively with your life, you would never question his "medical opinion" right? When you think about it, we've always had a fair amount of stress in our lives. Coming up though I can't recall even a single commercial advertising medications to treat *any* discomfort that may arise. But these days the moment you turn on the T.V there's a pill for depression, another one for ADD, a third for social anxiety disorder and an eighth for I.B.S.. These days there are more conditions than clouds in the sky, and most likely a little pill or two to make it all go away. There's the birth control pill, the morning after pill, night before pill, acid reflux pill etc, etc ... and enough pharmaceutical companies frothing at the mouth to keep you coming back to the drugstore for your next fix.

PARAPHERNALIA

Is there anything you *can't* make a bong out of? A coconut, apple, soda can, toilet paper dispenser? Many of my friends have a soft spot in their hearts for the holy "herb," some to the point of even growing their own crops in the basement, closet, or anywhere else outside of general traffic. In fact, now that I think about it most of my homies attended the University of Marijuana for at least a year or two. Some of them even go back for refresher courses every now and then. Truth is, even the good ganja has it's drawbacks. Aside from the short term memory loss and "munchies," you never really know what the hell you're smoking or what it's sprayed with. But who really cares? All we're looking for is a little bit of relief to make everything alright. Even if it only lasts fifteen or twenty minutes.

Sex, drugs and rock n' roll have always been part of the four major food groups in the American (and Amerfrican) diet. People with money do drugs. People with no money do drugs. And it's not just doctors, lawyers, professional athletes, politicians or actors that have the sweet tooth. Today it's soccer moms, bartenders, secretaries, high school teachers, nurses … the list goes on and on. Drugs affect all areas of society so to declare "WAR ON DRUGS" means declaring war on your sister, business partner, or God forbid your own Mama.

COLD TURKEY

When your car breaks down, you simply go to the auto parts place, buy the part you need and replace it. Then you drive off knowing that it's fixed. When YOU break down though, you put yourself through hell and high water just to admit that you have a problem in the first place. Then you go through the process of cleaning up your act, getting yourself together, making good decisions etc … In America you can beat most anything with money. That is, anything but a habit. A habit doesn't respond to deep pockets, other than draining 'em dry. Aside from that, you're money's no good here bruh. Of course if you're a movie star your cash may make your detox a bit more comfortable and the food tastier, but it won't take away that craving. You see, everybody's different. I know people who can pull an all-nighter and look like they got a full eight hours of sleep the next day. I also know a guy who gets blitzed off one beer. Some people can only take their medicine in small doses while others develop such a tolerance that it seems as if they could go on forever.

But let's take a look at how drugs affect Black people and the Amerfrican in particular. First of all, as a people we are extremely sensitive. I don't know if it's a physiological thing or just a reaction to all the bull***t we go through. Either way, s**t hits us hard jack! So hard that in many instances it's nearly impossible to pick ourselves up from off the canvas. Drugs are nothing new to the Black community that's for sure. We all know that. Heroin, powder cocaine, crack and ecstasy are as much a part of the Black experience as basketball and hip hop. And we feed off (and get hooked on) the adrenaline just as much as the next group. But the major misconception in society is that Black folks are the biggest users and dealers around. To me this is a joke, and a bad one at that. EVERY community is affected in different ways. Believe that. And we all have people close to us that have been affected, either as users/abusers, dealers, or victims of senseless crime. At one point or another most of us have even been forced to choose between trying/selling a certain substance or other. Like I said, it's almost like a crap shoot. But if you crap out in this game you're likely to lose a lot more than your shirt! When we become hooked on whichever drug gives us that OOMPH! we develop even more personalities than the ones we've already adopted just to make it through the week. "Why am I drinking whiskey for breakfast?" Your guess is as good as mine brotha. But it's probably a safe bet that you're trying to forget about something or other that's been on your mind for some time. Different stimuli make Blacks "tweak" than say, Asians. But one thing's for sure. If you do develop a "jones" you can't seem to get a grip on, the longer you put off dealing with it the sooner it'll come back to bite you in the ass …

Bottom Line: JUST SAY NO! If that's too hard then just say not right now. Making good choices ain't always easy people, especially when you're just tryin' to have a good time. And these days most people really aren't thinking about the future, they're just trying to make it through the day! So they take various substances to escape whatever they're afraid of or don't want to face. All I can say is BE CAREFUL brothers and sisters, 'cause the truth about it is that the same things that make you laugh, feel free, uninhibited, brave and the life of the party tonight can (and probably will) make you cry next week, month or year. Believe that.

9

THE MONEY SHOT

"Somewhere between love and madness lies ..."

The money shot? That's right my fellow "deviants," PORN. Which unless you've been trapped underneath a rock or living on the Moon for the past decade or so you've been exposed to in some way, shape or form. Also known as smut, blue movies, "that garbage" or the new "crack." But just what is it about this tantalizing, pulsating form of entertainment that's got so many of us tuned in and turned out? Could it be that we've fallen head over heels in lust with the fantasy? Or perhaps we're just hell bent on recreating an old familiar feeling. Either way, heaven knows we're a long way from the days of the stray *Playboy/Penthouse/Hustler* magazine on the coffee table that's for sure. No my friends this drug is a whole new strain altogether kids. Believe that. Today's porn is the kinda s**t that makes folks tweak, wash up then come right on back for another hit. Over the last fifteen years or so it's swept the nation more than the Beatles' invasion of the 60's. And we love it twice as much. Boy, do we ever!!! It's alright you can admit it. I won't tell ...

GRANDMA: *Peaches, I am just too through with you right now girl! You know you was brought up better than that!*

PEACHES: *Maybe so Grandma, but it's different now. You had your* *toys, we have ours, that's just the way it is these days.*

GRANDMA: *Hush up your mouth girl!! Before I make you go wash it out. In this family we don't talk like that and we sure as hell don't tolerate that kind of nasty behavior you hear me chile?*

PEACHES: *Yes, I hear you Grandma but everybody's doin' it ...*

Peaches is right. Unless some kind of great flood or other natural disaster reigns down to wash the Earth of all this filth, it looks like porn is here to stay folks. And it's getting more and more hardcore every day. But what is our intense fascination with midgets, farm girls, "barely legals" and "big naturals" really all about? For some of us, it's just a passing phase that we eventually outgrow and graduate to our next craving or aversion. For many more of us it's a weekly, daily, or hourly thing (like any other drug). And along the way we've quickly become geek monsters and goop gobblers of epic proportions, complete with the moans, groans and licking of lips. Pornography these days is more like a low budget slasher film, the more we cringe the more we find ourselves glued to the tube. You'd be amazed at what goes on behind closed doors in America. On second thought, you'd probably get excited. The point is, we've reached a time where nothing is off limits, no "holes" are barred, and everything is acceptable regardless of how twisted. These days the sex-o-meter is off the charts. And the overtones are seen everywhere from music videos to car commercials. Soap opera stars jump in and out of the sack faster than you can say one night stand. Then the commercial comes on with the dirty blonde purring "What goes on in Vegas stays in Vegas." You turn off the boob tube, flick on the radio and hear another female pushing some new cream, herb, lotion or potion promising heightened pleasure, stamina and increased sensitivity. And don't forget that thirty day risk free trial and money back guarantee! This land of "head or tails" has led us to believe that it's all about gettin' it up, keepin' it hard, and makin' it last forever. But how did our view of

sexuality practically overnight become synonymous with the obliga-
tory "happy ending?"

Porn is like cereal. You've got your favorite(s), yet you're still curious as to the different brands on the shelf. But unlike your morning
Cap n' Crunch which could land you a cavity or two, a serious porn
"jones" could cost you a whole lot more than just a filling. But no
matter, your secret stash still keeps growing by leaps and bounds every
week or so. But I'm still trying to understand how this industry has
become so accepted in society that you now have "porn stars" crossing
over into mainstream movies strictly on the basis of their "performance" in titles like *A** Cream Pie* and *Face Invaders.* Of course it's
more or less harmless to check out a flick or two every once in a while
by yourself or with your significant other. But we all know it's gone
way past that point by now. When I was young pornography was a
novelty. Or maybe I was just young. However these days you can buy
a detachable stripper pole for your rec room. You could also find your
co-worker (or boss) enjoying a little freaky deaky in their cubicle!
There are many levels of porn out here today, from "girly mags" to
strip clubs, "massage" parlors to escort services and of course the hardcore scene. The problem is (as it always is) that there is very little control over what is available to the kids which leaves them vulnerable to
images they have no business being exposed to. And it's only getting
worse.

Not surprisingly, the origins of pornography can be traced all the
way back to ancient Greek society. Deriving from the Greek words
porne ("prostitute") and graphein ("to write"), the word pornography
originally referred to any work of art or literature dealing with sex and
sexual themes. The Greeks used these themes in their songs and kinky
festivals, and the ancient Romans painted pornographic pictures on
the walls in the ancient city of Pompeii. What separates pornography
from obscenity or erotica however is quite simple (in theory).
Obscenity is determined as anything society deems sexually immoral

and therefore can be punishable in a court of law. In this country, for example, obscene sexual acts might include sex with farm animals, corpses, or underage children. In other words, that "hardcore" s**t. Erotica is also considered sexually explicit writing or graphic images, the difference being that it shows men and women on equal terms in the exchange. So, in a legal sense, pornography can only be considered illegal if it is judged to be obscene. But in the real world we all know that when a child views such material it can alter his impressionable mind and behavior forever. Matter of fact a good friend of mine told me her first introduction to porn was through her own father. He apparently had a fetish for Asian orgies. Well one day she happened to uncover Daddy's little stash and proceeded to stick it in the ol' VCR. Remember those? Anyway, she told me just how much of an effect this had on how she looked at men, women and sex in general. And how being exposed to the porn made it difficult to sustain a healthy relationship for any period of time in adulthood. I can only imagine ... See, what most people don't realize is that it's not natural to be intimate with a complete stranger. Unless you're on T.V (soap operas, feature films, or porn) of course. You really have to be careful these days folks.

IF IT'S ALRIGHT FOR THE PRESIDENT ...

But what's wrong with a little "shooby dooby" anyway? There's a thin line between a freak and a "perv" and most of us tiptoe on that line every day. As a young kid coming up my sex education came in the form of lunch table talk and locker room chatter. My parents never taught me about the birds and the bees. I'm sure they were uncomfortable so they just decided it'd be easier to avoid the subject altogether. That didn't stop me from finding out on my own. I was around eleven when it all began. Started out with the standard girly magazines; *Hustler, Penthouse, Oui, Cheri* ... I already had a sizable baseball and basketball card collection up to this point. But being the average horned out preteen without so much as a clue to how to my "nuts" were even supposed to hang, this was a whole new ball game.

Naturally I ran with it. I've always been a good athlete. Kept my stash in a dingy red gym bag under the bed or the back of my closet, and pretty soon I was like a junkie on a weekend bender. Rather harmless I suppose, aside from the occasional wet dream and one track mind. From the age of around twelve to sixteen I became more and more infatuated with the female form and the many things she could do with it. My harmless "habit" became pretty heavy although probably no more or less than that of my classmates, and high school became the phase of experimenting with girls and tryin' to get the most practice as possible. Back then we didn't have the Internet so porn was not exactly at our fingertips as is the case today. Thank goodness! It was more of a recreational thing than anything else in my eyes. Today is a whole new world my friends, but I'm sure you already know this. See, the same things we claim to despise are the same things we lust for. And this is the paradox. What are we supposed to do with all of this sexual energy that we all have pent up inside? When we can't find constructive ways to release or channel it where does it go?

One thing's for sure. Crack is "wack." But the truth is we live in a sexually repressive culture, with men generally acknowledged as superior to women. It's also true that WOMEN don't exist within the gang-bang world of pornography. Just tits, ass, and p*$$y. Our infatuation with the kitty cat and all things freaky deaky leads to some of the most unsavory attitudes towards women you could imagine. But that's how it is today. And after all, don't women love surprises? Sure they do, especially those that cum in big packages. But that doesn't make it right. And I know some females who enjoy watching porn just as much as the fellas. Basically it is what it is my friends, the perfect microcosm of American society. To be fair though, porn is nothing but a recreational mind f**k for most. At least in my humble opinion. But who really knows? Just fifty years ago pushing the envelope was a skirt that rose above the knee! But things have changed. And like most other sectors of society the porn industry is filled with a number of disturbing double standards. Women are seen as dirty, nasty, filthy etc ... while men are called "the man", stud, Gigolo, Mandingo and so forth. Not only that, what do you call a man that is overtly confident or sure of himself? Cocky. If he displays courage or guts in a particular situation then he's got "balls." But just like crack, or any other drug for that matter it's not as simple as Just Say No. There's a thin line between pleasure and pain, as the words we use to describe sexual intercourse further attest to; f#@k, screw, bang, smash, beat etc ... which all have surprisingly violent connotations.

The Black woman, in particular is adversely affected by this objectification of the feminine gender. In most porn flicks she is pounced upon like a piece of raw meat, only with less respect. And don't forget to call her "Black bitch" for good measure. But considering her invaluable position as nurturer and backbone of the Black family, her participation and dehumanization in these smut films is potentially devastating. And not only to herself. You see, the women in our lives have always been there for us. Yet the Black woman in particular has always been the easiest way to weaken the Black male. Take her outside of her character (and our lives) and the effects are devastating, which only makes her participation in porn even more tragic. But it's also predictable. Or in the words of noted author and novelist Alice Walker:

"For centuries the black woman has served as the primary pornographic "outlet" for white men in Europe and America. We need only think of the black women used as breeders, raped for the pleasure and profits of their owners. We need only think of the license the "master" of the slave women enjoyed. But, most telling of all, we need only study the old slave societies of the South to note the sadistic treatment at the hands of white "gentlemen" of beautiful "quadroons and octoroons" who became increasingly (and were deliberately bred to become) indistinguishable from white women and were the more highly prized as slave mistresses because of this. (Walker 1981, 42)

So you see this objectification of the female gender and the Black woman in particular is directly linked to the image of women from the time of slavery up until now. In other words, white men love themselves some "brown sugar." And white chicks?

Well, as an equal opportunity observer I would be remiss if I failed to include my "paler" sisters into the equation. How could I forget about you Peggy Sue? Caucasian females have always been infatuated with the Black female figure as well as the male apparatus. You hear all the time "Girl I wish I had a bigger butt" amongst white girls. Black women by the age of sixteen usually have "junk in the trunk" and rarely have this problem. It is well known that women are extremely self-conscious when it comes to their physical appearance. To make matters worse we live in a society where appearance goes a long way. Some women feel out of place for having *real* breasts! Back in the day girls with less "up top" would pad their bras with tissue to make their breasts look bigger and fuller. These days you have women saying "Later for that wonder bra" and spending thousands of dollars to push that C up to a DD. Somewhere in her mind she feels that having bigger breasts will suddenly make her feel better about herself and more attractive to men. Maybe it will, maybe it won't, but for some reason you see this phenomenon primarily in the Caucasian community. And they're getting them younger and younger. College girls, and in some cases even high school girls not even eighteen are saving up their allowance and pocket money for a pair of new "boo-bies." Next day they're flashing them for the cameras and a bunch of horned out teens during Spring Break. And guess where they're receiving these messages that bigger is so much better? That's right my friends, PORN. 'Cause the first two things they notice when they watch it are the dimensions of the woman's breasts and the size of the man's "tool." But then again we're all obsessed with the flesh. How many times have you been walking down the street and noticed some overly muscle bound down dude looking like Superman from the waist up. Arms all bulging, chest blaring out from beneath his sleeveless shirt exaggerating his physique like the president? Then you notice his skinny, birdlike legs that make him look more like Popeye after the spinach. Point is, we all perceive ourselves as coming up short in one area or another. So we compensate in very odd ways for our imaginary lack of whatever. We've all heard the saying "Beauty is only skin deep" (but ugly is to the bone) which means what I find attractive in a woman may not necessarily be what the next man finds appealing and vice versa. And what's so wrong with that? Why can't we just be OKAY with how the good Lord created us? Oh no. Not in today's microwave culture. What we do is accept whatever images are deemed beautiful and tailor our "look" around that. This is why you have so many health and fitness clubs springing up filled with all types of machines where you can work on those traps, lats, pecs, and abs. And in case you didn't know 99.9 % of what we do is to impress the opposite sex. But it's getting out of hand folks. With all the plastic surgery, liposuction, stomach stapling and tummy tucking going on you could come home and not even recognize your own wife! Now ladies I can understand if you've had a couple children and them "kiddies" aren't exactly sittin' where they used to. How can I be mad at you for wanting a little help with the merchandise? But we all know a little bit of anything can become addictive, and with some of these video vixens and porn starlets as your point of reference you could find yourself doped up at the doctor's office searching for your own nipple! I'm kidding, but living up to the fantasy is hard. And just because you paid three thousand dollars for the procedure doesn't necessarily mean you'll be comfortable enough with your body to keep the lights on next time you do the nasty.

So the other evening I was in my room doing "research" for this text, and so I popped in a copy of *"Cape Spear"* for reference material. Boy was I in for some surprises! Long gone are the days of grainy black and white images shot in sleazy motel rooms where the "actors" don't bother to remove their black socks and house shoes for the sake of the camera. Enter the lush, lavish sets, tropical locales and drop dead gorgeous almost cover girls and guys geeked up on Viagra and steroids that make up today's smut industry.

"Once again, what's wrong with a little hanky panky anyway?"

Nothing. As long as you know the difference between fantasy and reality. What's the difference? Reality is a romantic candlelit dinner at your favorite restaurant with your honey bun after a long work week. Appetizers of course, soft music, pinot grigio and grilled salmon followed by a leisurely stroll in the moonlight. And a little "rabbit dancin'" for dessert (once the kids are asleep of course). Fantasy is comin' home to two girls in pigtails, high heels and garter belts talkin' 'bout "We've been waiting all night for you baby! …" How can you compete with that? And the puppet masters of the industry know this. Still, we all love to live a bit on the outside, just a bit though, not too much. You can't live at Disneyworld. But you can visit for the day, take in the rides and keep your hands in the air while you await the big drop. This craze is about more than a big butt and a smile though. It's a billion dollar industry and a highly marketable worldwide commodity that has quickly become synonymous with popular culture. You can order it in the penthouse suites of five star international hotels. Or you can download it onto your good 'ol laptop. And if you don't have one there's always your local "superstore" where you can pick up whatever it is you need to scratch that itch. These days they're more convenient than the 24 hr. drive-thru. But the subconscious element to pornography is almost as fascinating as the economic/financial aspect. What drives people to suppress and obsess, rewind and fast forward to whatever gets their "rocks off" is indeed the fantasy. And indeed it's all about the fantasy. Tension and release. That's why watching a DVD or videotape requires your undivided attention. That means no cell phone, radio, or other impediments to the inevitable climax. Viewing porn requires complete concentration, at times reaching the level of hypnosis. If you've ever found yourself glued to the screen for an excessive amount of time you know exactly what I'm talkin' about. But once you've had your fill of your particular fetish, whether its schoolgirls in plaid skirts, midgets, clowns or "heavy-weights," you eventually have to step back into reality. But let's be honest folks. What normal red-blooded male wouldn't want to "get it on" with two or three freaked out bunnies with no strings attached? Many guys would think they'd done died and gone to heaven! Sorry ladies, that goes for your man too. Of course he'd never admit it but trust me on this one. Don't worry though. It's really not personal, just pleasurable. And believe me I understand that two can play that game as well. The point I'm tryin' to make is that fantasy and reality go hand in hand. And this is why pornography is so lucrative. And also why so many "celebrities" are making a killing just by releasing grainy low budget homemade movies of themselves gettin' busy.

So it's only natural that the fear of a Black penis would extend to the porn world where the image of the big Black stud or "Mandingo" is one of the most recognizable (and mass marketed) in all of the industry. I'm sure you're familiar with the pictures of the "well hung" Black stud plastered all over the covers of DVD's and videotapes in your local sex shop. This sexual tension is played out to the hilt with ridiculous titles like *"Horny Blonde Brotha Lovas," "Philadelphia Jones and the Temple of Poon,"*and *Dark Meat 18.* Talk about racial profil-ing! Even the pimp aesthetic is taken to another level in the warped world of smut. Nevertheless due to the well known urban legend regarding the size and potency of the Black "package" the industry has found yet another ingenious method of perpetuating the stereotype of the brainless Black brute ready and willing to satisfy all "cummers." But what exactly is it about this "wood," I mean word and its many aliases that has so many folks enamored and utterly infatuated by? Psychologically, and in most societies the penis is the primary meta-phor for manhood, and the stature of one's "member" conjures up either feelings of superiority or inferiority depending on where one stands. This is a topic that's been buried in mystique and rarely dis-cussed openly for obvious reasons. Over the years Caucasians especially have developed a complex when it comes to the question of size and its importance in the bedroom. That is why it is only their faces you see on the E.D and penile enhancement commercials. And white women have always been the recipient of the often asked question; "Is it really true what they say about Black guys?" Be that as it may, amongst men the subject is one that for all intents and purposes remains a personal issue. So the last place any dude is looking while draining "the weasel" is over at the dude in the urinal next to him. We just don't get down like that. But white men find many other creative ways to express their manhood and flaunt their relatively comfortable position in society. Some of these include the acquisition of toys such as T-top Corvettes, Harley Davidsons, big fat Cuban cigars, and flexing their "muscle" in the workplace. The Amerfrican on the other hand is ogled with awe by women of all races and disdained by white boys who suffer from this "penis envy." Therefore there is much sexual tension that simmers beneath the surface of society which many of us feel but can't quite put our fingers on. It's almost like a racial tug of war. And although every woman has her own particular preference when it comes to what turns her on there can be no denying the mystique which surrounds the Black sexual organ. I mean, just look at the words we use to describe it: "wood," "pipe," "tool," "bone," "sword," "sausage," "magic stick …" Need I go on? It's funny, but at the end of the day the image we've come to accept as representative of Black men (especially in porn) does more to emasculate us when it comes to attaining true power in the real world. It only gives those with the real power more room to create caricatures and belittle the intelligence of some our sharpest MINDS. Remember King Kong? Well these days King "*Schlong*" has made his way into the bedrooms of millions of you horny toads yet he has made little to no progress when it comes to collective organization and unity amongst his own. Think about it. So ultimately the real question becomes; At what point did the Black man lose his true powers of creativity and expression? The answer? HE DIDN'T!!! He only misplaced it. And herein lies the dilemma he faces of trying to find his true "house keys."

"When the moment comes, will you be ready?"

The commercial was so warm and inviting, two mature lovers on a romantic getaway vacation at the beach, walking hand in hand and staring lovingly into each other's eyes. Serenaded by smooth jazz and the deeply relaxing tone of the voice-over guy, it continues to show the couple at dinner and a show, giggling and laughing like little kids. Then, after the narrator runs down the potential side effect as being minor, he again praises the drug for it's thirty six hour convenience, so "If she's not ready now, there's always tomorrow night." Then, as the cozy saxophone sings and the man and woman embrace, the voice coolly comes back on with; "Serious side effects may include sudden loss of vision," followed by "Consult your physician if erection lasts for more than four hours." WHAT! Finally it's "When the moment comes, will you be ready?" For a six hour boner? Uhm, I'm good thanks. But we continue to be constantly bombarded by these advertisements telling us we don't measure up, whether it's during halftime of the Super Bowl, A.M talk radio, or in the form of pharmaceutical spam on our desktop. "Keeping it up" is the new national anthem. Doctors say that as a man ages, gradually his physical vitality decreases along with his staying power between the sheets. This is only natural. So why all the high anxiety and constant pressure to be the "Energizer Bunny?"

CREATURES OF HABIT

We go online for everything from cheap airline tickets and good deals on flat screens to poker tournaments and live sex shows. These days everything is interactive. We do our banking, buy our music, books, and Christmas gifts on the computer. With the new technology practically anybody can have a "new friend" or arrange a discreet encounter. After all, we love anything where there's a bit of risk and danger involved. But there's a big difference between what's good to you and what's good FOR YOU. Back in the day, sticking your hand in the cookie jar would get you a whuppin' from Mama at best. These days you could end up on national T.V. in the center of a "sting" operation. The fear of being found out not only excites us but drives us even further to fulfill our cravings. It has never been so easy to "get off" as it is today. A double-click here, right click there will get you exactly where you need to go. And once you arrive, the world is literally in the palm of your hand. Prompts for this, downloads for that, there is a virtual onslaught on our left and right brains as soon as we click ENTER making it easy to get tangled up. And even if you happen to click on a porn site by "mistake" you gotta damn near go through hell just to get back to where you were without a million more pop-up ads coming up! Just make sure you have your credit card handy. Then there's that television show, the one where they catch the online predators on the prowl. You know the one where the forty-something "gentleman," screen name "Bone Daddy 69" approaches the house with a big fat grin on his face. Under his arm is a bag containing a fifth of vodka, cold cuts and "Rough Rider" condoms. Oh, and a dildo. Apparently this evening "Boner's" got a hot date with a sexy 13 yr. old he's been chatting with online. When he realizes something's just not right he suddenly makes a move to the door to leave. Then comes the investigative reporter; "So, just what exactly did you have in mind with a 13 yr. old sir?" "You're how old?" "Forty seven" Bone Daddy replies. You do know that what you're doing is against the law right?" Bone Daddy: "I swear to you sir, I know it's wrong but please … just please! I got a wife and three kids!! You know how it goes from here. There was a time you had to go to the back of your local City Paper to set up a discreet encounter. But now it's "Send me a pic baby so I can see if you match the image in my mind!" "And make sure it's a recent one too." But what's even more disturbing are the amount of pedophiles running around all over town. Back in the day a child molester hung around the schoolyard waiting for his chance to "befriend" an unsuspecting child. These days he doesn't even have to leave his bedroom. Furthermore, the Internet is chock full of dating services, swingers' sites and straight up prostitution rings. And the clientele is far from just dirty old men and pimply faced teens. We're talkin' about "happily married" men (and women), couples who have been together for twenty years, deacons, dentists, and phys ed teachers. They usually make you verify you are over the age of eighteen to enter, but even a five year old can check YES! And if you don't have the net at home you can in many instances just log on at your local public library! Tragically, many spouses have absolutely no clue that their significant other is leading such a double life. Most men in fact feel that chatting with "Diamond Princess" every day is no big deal, just a harmless flirtation. Like I said before maybe it is, maybe it isn't. But temptation is hard to resist. And only you know when you've crossed the line. It's just that most of you don't really care. All you're really interested in is the "money shot."

Bottom Line: The bottom line is nobody really wants to know what kind of moaning, groaning, panty sniffing high heel shoe fetish freak you are behind closed doors! What you do in the privacy of your own space is your personal business brothers and sisters. And as long as it's not hurting the kids and you're cool with it I guess I am too. Just remember that there really is a thin line between fantasy and obsession and try not to get caught up. If you do, seek help. Simple as that. There are hotlines all over the place that can wean you off the stuff. For the rest of you, enjoy yourselves and make sure you don't do anything that I wouldn't do. Good Luck ...

10

YOU ARE HEALED!/ TAKE ME TO YOUR LEADER

I was taught the two things you never, *ever* debate are politics and religion. But it took me a long time to understand just why. See, people are very passionate about their faith and political point of view. So if by chance you end up "discussing" either/or nine times out of ten you'll either hurt someone's feelings or end up making a new enemy or three. That's why I decided to make it easy on myself and condense these two sections into one to avoid all of that. A few general observations though. We are always told to think outside the box (wherever that is). That is until it comes to our perception of God and religion. Take religion for starters; thinking outside the box when it comes to faith or religious belief usually puts us directly in the line of fire or called all types of unmentionables. But why? It's almost as if looking for the Most High in any place but the church, mosque, synagogue or Bible Study is against the rules. We all know just by looking around us that God has infinitely more faces and places than we give Her credit for. Yet we limit our perspective to whichever religious system we either have grown up with or gravitated to at some point in life. The main theme remains constant throughout though; all we want is HAPPINESS! And only we can determine what this means for us individually in our particular circumstance. What would make you truly HAPPY? A million dollars? A wife/husband, two kids, big house and white picket fence? Would you feel happy then? God only knows. Most of us equate happiness with one or more of these things, yet when we finally obtain them we still find ourselves restless and in search of more to fill the void. In fact for many of you the "almighty dollar" has become your main source of joy and happiness. That's why you feel wonderful when you have some "Benjamins" in your pocket and "broke" when you don't. Money won't fix you, but it can give you more options. Meanwhile, we hear all the time that we're in the midst of spiritual warfare here on Earth, with opposing forces duking it out for control of our minds, bodies and souls and the truth will come to light on Judgement Day. It's true. What they usually leave out is the fact that every day is "Judgement Day." Think about it. First thing you do in the morning when you look in the mirror is judge yourself right? The spiritual warfare *we* put ourselves (and each other) through on a daily basis is enough in itself to make you lose your damn mind! I've often wondered if lasting happiness is even possible? True enough, I run into folks all the time who say "I'm doin' great man!" "Yeah life is good brotha!" Then the next time you see them it's like "Oh I'm doin' okay man." "Could be better, could be worse. Can't complain. Even if I did nobody would listen." How often have you heard this? Listen people. We all go through life's ups and downs. That's why most of us lean on a higher power to help us through the rough patches in the first place. But what is it that's making it so hard to be at ease people? Like you I'd love to see peace on Earth, goodwill toward man and so forth and so on. But all I seem to see these days is a lot of "high horsing" and finger pointing. The "MY GOD IS BETTER THAN YOURS!" complex is now definitely at its highest peak than I can ever recall in my lifetime. I often wondered why I never felt completely comfortable belonging to any of the "isms" that exist out here today. Then one day I finally realized that I didn't have to! I mean, have you ever considered how the world would look if there were NO religions all? Just a thought. But since that'll never happen (in our lifetime anyway) the least we could do is appreciate other folks' point of view and give them a chance to express themselves the way they're most comfortable. Yeah? Cool.

Bottom line: We all claim to be seekers of the truth, and most of us spend our whole lives trying to find it. We also have more answers to our questions than we give ourselves credit for. This knowledge in itself can take us further than any foot stompin,' hand clappin', or speakin' in tongues ever could. Can I get a witness???

TAKE ME TO YOUR LEADER

We don't know who the hell to trust anymore. But can you blame us? Every time we put our trust in men we either get taken for a ride or sold down the river. It's a shame, but we've learned how to grin, bear it and go on with our lives. Question? If someone came up and asked you to name three Black leaders who would they be? Take a minute or two, you'll probably need it. And I don't mean someone who just says all the right things but never comes through in the clutch. It was different before. Our elders had strong, visible leaders such as King, Malcolm, Garvey and the various writers, poets and activists of the Harlem Renaissance, Civil Rights, Pan-African and Black Power movements. Today however we seem to be lacking any kind of universal agenda, much less leadership. Just individual goals, dreams and money schemes. In my opinion most Amerfricans don't believe that a Black man is *capable* of leading them much less the entire nation. Meanwhile the baby boomers of yesterday are getting older and Generation X is next up to bat. I know that it's not as easy as just saying; "We're gonna fix this issue" or "We need to overhaul that one." Yet that's usually the first thing you hear coming out the mouths of our so-called leaders. But the real reason we feel like we have no one that represents us is very simple. We no longer represent OURSELVES! What I mean is that our work (jobs, occupations) and spare time for the most part only benefit us (and our small circle) financially or socially, leaving us with little time much less energy to develop any collective agenda or platform for change in the places where we need it the most.

RUN JESSE RUN!!!

Away that is … Just kidding folks, but if you ask people today (Black or white) they'd probably echo this sentiment. See, it used to be; "What have you done for me lately?" But now it's more like "What you gon' do for me right now!!! Who are we kiddin' folks? Do you really think America is ready for a Black president? S**t! *Black* people ain't even ready for a Black president!! And that's why you'll find any and every excuse not to vote for one. Of course it won't be because of the color of his skin. You'll think of another reason … See, the fear of a Black penis manifests itself in so many ways and cuts across all racial, social, economic and yes political lines. But how 'bout an Amerfrican president? Please. At least you'll be given the choice very soon. Just make sure you think carefully before pulling that lever.

JUST WIN BABY

Anyway, the fundamental problem that no one wants to address is that in order to be a politician you have to be an accomplished LIAR. Point blank. This is something you must understand. In politics honesty is simply not the best policy. And it's always easier to tell people what they want to hear than the truth of the matter. The truth of this matter is that Black folks have always had mixed emotions when it comes to politics. I wonder why? At the expense of sounding politically "erect," I mean correct, personally I believe it's because we still think that we need someone else to address *our* issues and solve *our* problems even though we have seen time and again this has never worked. We live in an extremely competitive society people. Even the water that we drink is a political decision. It's not just the two major political parties which have failed the people so miserably. It is our blind dependence and reliance on them that is the source of our condition. For some reason, we put more trust in elected officials and their campaign promises than we do our own common sense. Our threshold for accepting double talk, faulty "intelligence," and outright lies has reached an all time high and a gaping hole where the ninth ward used to be. Politicians misrepresent the facts, forget, or conveniently can't remember the sequence of events that just happened yesterday. Then, three months later the real story is "leaked" to the media and becomes fodder for the various media outlets and Sunday news programs. There is a general wariness of all things political these days, especially within the Black community. We're frustrated, and this is why at this point many of us could CARE LESS who sits in the Oval Office. We've come to the cold hard realization that it really and truly doesn't even matter anymore.

Bottom Line: We spend too much time agreeing with the wrong voices. This is why we are so easily led astray. We hand out our trust like we hand out Halloween candy, yet haven't even decided where we truly stand. Are we liberal? Conservative? Both?? Neither??? Do we feel like we are a part of the process or just in the way of the process? Truly represented or "pissed on?" Forget the politicians. We need to hold *each other* accountable for being gullible enough to fall for the "okey doke" in the first place! By now it's clear that whoever is pulling the strings doesn't want Black folks organized to begin with. But that doesn't mean we have to keep giving them the last laugh. Actions speak louder than words people. Don't just trust a spellbinding preacher or politician because they give you goose pimples and watery eyes. 'Cause at the end of the day the only person you can really put your trust in is YOU.

11

DOUBLE DRIBBLE

But who wants to think about all that heavy stuff every minute of the day? Sometimes we just want to "veg out," kick back, toss back a cold one and take in a good game. I gotta say though these days it's been hard for me to keep up with all the young bucks comin' into the league seein' as how barely any of 'em are stayin' in school more than a year or two. The game has changed a bit as well from the days of my youth. The players are more athletic, the uniforms are *a lot* baggier and the salaries much more lucrative. But although so much has changed in the game that I grew to love so much coming up, some things remain the same. The first thing an NBA player still gets once he makes it to "The League" is a new car and a white girl. I'm sorry, first he gets a house for his Mama then a white girl. Alright maybe that's going a little too far. But one thing's for certain; sports are the perfect microcosm of society and a barometer for the perplexing times we live in. The ebb and flow of the game keeps us glued to our seats, mesmerized by the high flying, lightning quick moves and grooves of those talented enough to make it to the pros. We secretly wish we could be in their shoes, pockets, and bedrooms if even for just a week (or three). Just imagine how it must feel to be "at the top of your game?" Truth is, most of us never reach the mountaintop of our respective professions so we applaud and admire those who've gone through the grueling two-a days, spring training, preseason and off-season workouts, not to mention the lifelong commitment and dedication it takes to rise to the top. And we all know what we'd have done if the ball had bounced just a little bit differently when we had our shot. But do we really? It's one thing to cop the latest Jordans, pull your socks up to your knees and imitate #23's patented baseline turnaround or AI's killer crossover. It's another thing entirely to maintain the discipline, work ethic, and perseverance necessary to shine before the glaring lights and cameras of the "big time." So we remain content wearing our favorite superstar's name on our backs, fronts, heads and feet.

Sometimes I wonder where my teammates are and what they're up to these days. I really do miss the good ole days man. The late 70's and 80's in particular when the game was pure and you could actually sit through the whole thing instead of just the fourth quarter. Man, was I a basketball junkie! Sure was, and proud of it too. I remember precisely when I got my first fix. It was the night Kareem was hurt and out of the lineup and a young, gangly rookie from Michigan State was forced to play all five positions (yes center too) in his place and ended up having one of the most legendary games in NBA history with 42 points, 15 rebounds and 7 assists. This same kid went on to make the term "triple double" a household term and pop more than his share of bubbly throughout his magical career. Didn't even matter that he'd done it against my favorite player in the league at the time, the Doctor, Julius "Dr. J" Erving and his Philadelphia 76ers. I was just a kid, and lanky as I could be with my socks pulled to my knees. I didn't really care what kinda sneakers I had on my feet, much less how much they cost. I just loved the game. In fact, for a while there, basketball was even my girlfriend. I ate, drank, slept, and dreamt about the game. Oh, don't act like you didn't do the same thing! Anyway, wasn't a day I got home from school that I couldn't be found at somebody's court or playground workin' on my jumper, free throws, and my cool ass pose. I'd mimic my mentors, puttin' myself in their socks, sneakers, jerseys and place. Mind you, this was the era of the gold chain, and these cats were actually allowed to wear their chains and medallions on the court. You shoulda seen these super smooth brothas lookin' all pimped out, sportin' their hip 'fros wit' their gold glistenin' all over the place (this was before platinum). I mean, can you even imagine in today's game the sight of these flashy young bucks barely out of high school running up and down the court flashin' their $100,000 platinum, diamonds, and rubies all over the floor! Then all of a sudden a brotha's chain gets snagged on the next man's jersey or ripped from his neck as he flies to the hoop for a reverse jam! All of a sudden brothas start to brawlin' and scrappin' like they fightin' for freedom or somethin.' I can only imagine ... But then again, nobody really wants to lose all that paper over a misunderstanding. No harm, no foul right? And the last thing we need to see on the news is "Riot breaks out on the court." More at 11:00. Thank goodness the whole chain thing was scrapped before it got out of hand. But with all the undertones of thuggism that has seeped into this beautiful sport you may, like myself be paying close attention to what they're not tellin' us. So, as usual the question remains; "What's *really* goin' on here?"

"Here's what I think Coach. I think it's time to let these young boys know who's really runnin' shit, that's what I think. They startin' to get a liitle too comfortable with all that guaranteed money we givin' em. And everyone knows they don't know how to act once they get a bunch of money ... Guess lifelong financial security, a new car, shoe contract, house in the hills, and all the weed they can possibly smoke ain't enough to keep these boys from f***in' up our investment. I know they're rebellious by nature, but g**damn! Well I got somethin' for 'em. Yes indeedy, best believe I got somethin' for 'em alright."

WHO'S YOUR DADDY?

The current dictat ... I mean commissioner of the National Basketball Association must be climbing the walls of his plush, swanky office as we speak. I mean, he's really got a problem on his hands unless he nips it in the bud real quick. Young, strapping Black athletes in superb physical shape, threatening all that advertising revenue and jeopardizing the marketability of the most lucrative sport on the planet. No wonder they can afford to pay these young boys virtually unheard of salaries just to bounce a basketball up and down the court and throw it into a goal. Look how much they're making off of them! And those floor seats don't come cheap either. Depending on which city you happen to be in, they can go into the low four digit range. Easy. And every time the camera pans to these well coveted courtside seats, one thing remains consistent. The folks sitting in them look absolutely nothing like the players that they come to see. Unless, of course it's the hottest rapper and his lady who happen to be in the house. But still, what is the commissioner to do to stem the tide on all the unsportsmanlike conduct, questionable "character" guys and "thug lifers" and still keep his investment and cash cow intact?

*"Commish, maybe you should make the players wear suits to the games? Maybe that'd get 'em to straighten up and fly right. I dunno, I mean none of the other sports from football and baseball to hockey have a dress code but I just think that it'd keep 'em from looking all thugged out during press conferences. All this bling bling is **not** a good look for the sport."*

Now this is not the first time the "Godfather" has been faced with a tough decision or two during his seemingly lifetime position as basketball Don. During the mid to late 70's and early 80's another potential catastrophe threatened to give the game a serious "black eye." This time, ironically it came in the form of a white snowstorm. As in most areas of society at the time, from the recording and motion picture industry to the boardrooms of corporate America, cocaine was blowing its way through the sports world with avalanche like intensity. This blizzard forced many of the game's brightest stars into rehab, many others into early retirement before the age of thirty, and countless more onto the street. When "blow" began to infiltrate and saturate the locker rooms of established NBA franchises and high profile superstars began to fall victim to it's seductive allure, the "boss" was forced to seriously put his foot down and institute a drug policy which included a potential "blackball" from the league after three strikes. Ironically, in other sports such as baseball with similar escalating drug problems, players were given three, four, and in some cases many more chances to return to the field.

So we are faced with finding new solutions for old problems. You see, the NBA is the only sport of the big three where the human body is virtually uncovered and not camouflaged by padding or headgear. This only adds to the visual intensity of seeing these young Black "studs" out on center court. It is also the only sport in which you are so close to the action, the floor seats being just a few feet behind the bench allowing one to hear the action audibly as well as follow it visually. So when these bench clearing brawls take place, it's almost like a barroom brawl where virtually anything can happen. But let's be for real. Do the league suits really think these cats are just gonna lose their minds, run up into the stands and take over Madison Square Garden? Funny thing is, when you see the same brawls and fisticuffs exhibited in the National Hockey League on a nightly basis, it is universally accepted as being part of the game. Go figure. And let's not start on Major League Baseball, where even the hint of a pitcher throwing at a batter is enough to draw both teams onto the field with even the coaches wanting in on the action. But when you begin to compare and contrast these three hugely popular sports the picture starts to become much clearer. And you see that the only glaring difference between the three is not the level of violence which is consistent across the board, but the racial makeup of the sport itself. In other words, b-ball (for the most part) is **Black.**

"Good Lord, first it was the tattoos, then it was the damn cornrows. We could make 'em cut their hair eh? … Okay maybe that's takin' things a little too far. But could somebody please tell me why these guys always have to make a damn scene everywhere they go?"

And ownership is white, which throughout our brief but storied time on the shores of North America has not always been the most convenient arrangement if you dig what I'm sayin.' And yes, it is encouraging to see Black athletes (and now rappers) becoming partial owners of NBA franchises, but the scales are still far from balanced. But back to our old friend "The Commish" and these new rules of engagement. Does he think fans really care about what the players wear to the gym? I mean seriously brothers and sisters, I understand that these days image is everything, but do you really believe that people are attending games less than in the past because they are turned off by cornrows and designer shades? Maybe. But this "anti-establishment" look is also the very same reason that millions of folks (white and Black), and probably your son or daughter can relate and are drawn to these world class athletes to begin with.

And then there was M.J. Ah yes, the man that literally had wings to fly. And suddenly it was, "If I could be like Mike." But when you dig deeper into this brilliant advertising fraud you see that there is always a trade-off when it comes to the Amerfrican's quest to reach that rarefied air of power so often dangled before his face like a carrot on a string. Yes children, be like Mike. But what does being like Mike *really* mean? It means be cool baby, be colorless and most importantly be QUIET! Because the last thing that the NBA wants you to be in this golden age of go for yours sadly enough is a nuisance. But just make sure you buy them Nikes. At $150 a pair. In fact, Air Jordan's were among the first sneaker of any kind that were over one hundred dollars at that point in time. But they would set the bar for what was to come. And why was Mike able to rise so meteorically into the corporate stratosphere, becoming the first athlete to be marketed worldwide to such a degree that his Air Jordan brand to this day remains the standard for quality basketball apparel? Could it be that he wasn't a thug? No tattoos on the neck of 'ol #23. No sir. But let's face it folks, having an abundance of tattoos on one's body has never been synonymous with thuggery. Just look at the punk rock/heavy metal bands out here and you can see that these guys are never referred to in this manner. They're "artists …" yet literally have hundreds of tattoos (and various piercings) plastered all over their bodies as well. They also have no problem whatsoever trashing hotel rooms, drugging it up, abusing women etc etc … Yet they are never ever labeled thugs. I guess sports is different though. S**t, half of America has tattoos so we know that simply being "tatted up" doesn't equate to thuggism. Maybe even your daughter has a couple in a few choice places herself. Is she a thug too? No, brothers and sisters, what makes your average Amerfrican NBA player who just happens to get caught up in the occasional courtside skirmish a gangsta thug is the fact that he is young, Black, and listens to hip hop music. Oh, and one more thing; he just happens to be way richer than *you*. Period.

So what is left? How can the NBA level off the playing field and make the league more "inclusive?" Well, my friends, that's easy. Diversify. Internationalize the game. The truth of the matter is that for the last several years the league has been on a mission to spread the religion of basketball throughout the four corners of the Earth. Well, not really. More like to European countries such as Croatia, Serbia, Yugoslavia, even China. But you rarely hear of the NBA diversifying to the cozy continent of Africa where you'd probably find the most talented athletes to take the game to new heights. Now be honest, if you, as a business owner were looking for the best possible product to put on the floor of an NBA team, where would you look first; Prague or Nigeria? But this fear of a black penis is understandable considering the fact that more Black ex-players are moving into coaching positions, front office jobs, and yes, ownership. Hopefully this trend will inspire a more unified voice, and one which accurately reflects the racial makeup of the league that I grew up with and gave me some of the fondest memories of my youth.

Listen folks, anyone with a half a brain can see that the league is too Black. There's an old saying in the community that goes "Too

Black, Too Strong." As the big, tough, rebellious, and yes slave image is plastered all over your plasma screen, the visual becomes uncomfortable just as it must have been when the colonialists encountered the strong, towering African hundreds of years ago. Unified strength inspires uneasiness because of it's potential implications. A large group of young, wealthy, CONSCIOUS anybodies willing to work together for a common cause is a threat to the existing power structure.

"Boss, they're just gettin' younger and younger. They're raw, untamed (I mean) untrained and just not ready to play on this level … Sh*t, these kids are barely outta high school for Christ's sake! And half of 'em never been to class a day in their freakin' life! I think we should really consider an age limit boss. Let 'em know who's really in charge here …"

Are you kiddin' me? Tennis has no problem whatsoever allowing fourteen year olds to turn professional. In fact, tennis organizations sponsor camps which bring teenage boys and girls in to learn and be taught by professionals not only how to play the game but how to adjust to the whirlwind lifestyle off the court. Is that because the majority of tennis players on the circuit are European? I'm sorry, but I'd rather just call a spade a spade man. Thank God for the Williams sisters. Anyhow, we've learned to take our victories in baby doses. Over the years our perception of freedom has been reduced to "the first to do this or the first to do that." "First Black man to break the color line in baseball." "First Amerfrican quarterback to win a Super Bowl." "First two Black coaches to go head to head in a Super Bowl." "First Amerfrican coach to win a Super Bowl." First Black man to win an Oscar for Best Actor." First Amerfrican in space." See what I'm sayin?

Bottom Line: I know it's just a game folks. But sports have always been a gauge of social change in America, and way after the results have been placed on the scoreboard. We've always raised the bar in terms of performance. Now let's see how much longer it takes for us to raise the stakes. Truth is, athletes are bought and sold to the highest bidder (team owner) each and every day. The only difference is today's athletes make more money than is humanly possible to spend. But you better believe that they are still considered the owner's property. Remember the '68 Olympics when the two brothers raised their Black fists in the air in protest of inequality and social injustices at home (and abroad). This simple gesture is still remembered forty years later. Why? Because they were unafraid to take a stand on social issues regardless of the consequences. Bear in mind they could have been shot as soon as they stepped off the plane for this, but they had the courage to put it all on the line for what they truly believed in. Today's Black athlete has been rendered impotent when it comes to expressing his opinion outside of the gymnasium or football stadium for fear of losing his financial security. But think about this, if even 75% of athletes pooled their vast resources together for a common cause, who knows, you might see more "colored faces" in the Louisiana Superdome next season when them "Saints go marching in."

12

D.W.B

So you're headed home from another mind numbing day at the office, lost in deep thought and seriously contemplating your future. The cool light drizzle has quickly become a fierce downpour causing you to seek the nearest cover. As you try to outrun the elements you notice a small, odd looking pouch on the ground before your feet. You take a look around, slowly reach down and pick the pouch up to see what's inside. From the moment you loosen its top you spot the neat stack of crisp, green, "dead presidents" protruding from the opening. Quite naturally the rush you feel is off the charts, your heart skipping two, three beats as you try to play it cool. Knowing the bank is right around the corner only heightens your excitement and bumps your mind into fifth gear. Outwardly you remain calm, glancing both ways, scoping your surroundings and considering your next move. Then you:

a) Close the pouch, place it on the ground where you found it and head on home to the family.

b) Stuff the pouch into your backpack along with the rest of your things and keep it moving.

c) Dial 911/take the bag directly to the police.

Or

d) Act "surprised," grab a couple wads of the cash then start yelling at anyone within earshot; "He went *THAT WAY!!!*" "What'd he look like?"

"Short Black guy with dreadlocks, he was wearing a dark sweat suit and white sneakers …"

What happens next my friends depends on which of these options you chose. And although this is a fictional scenario it's not quite as far fetched as you may think. Each moment the decisions we make determine our future and quality of life. And the level of our consciousness plays a big part in these decisions. But back to the story and what my research uncovered. Not surprisingly, most of you chose **(b)**, your reason being;

"I work hard, take care of my responsibilities and don't complain. 'Bout time I caught a break."

So even though the front of the pouch clearly reads in bold print: **"NATIONAL BANK," Please Contact Authorities/Return Immediately If Found**, at this point your mind has already hit overdrive. So much so that by the time your key hits the front door you've already paid off the bill collector, bought your dream car and one-way tickets to your tropical paradise. To be fair, some of you chose **(a)**, telling yourself;

"It doesn't belong to me man, just leave it alone."

And a few of you even selected **(c)**;

"Maybe they'll give me a reward or something for being honest."

Maybe. But it was the number of you who chose (**d**) that really blew my mind. On second thought, it's not all that surprising considering the day and age we live in. But what happens when there's videotape?

It's like this y'all. The same thing that's happening to the same brother in Philly is happening to the same brother in D.C. is happening to the same brother in New York is happening to the same brother in Atlanta is happening to the same brother in Los Angeles is happening to the same brother in Chicago is happening to the same cat in Florida and on and on and on … and they all end up going to the same place. But where is the accountability when the men and women sworn to protect and serve the community abuse their oath and go on their own "rampage?" In America Black life has been devalued. So much in fact that when for instance a young Black male is shot fifty times on his wedding day we tend to go into temporary shock and disbelief screaming "Bloody Murder!" and "We ain't gonna take this no more!" And that is where it stops. After two days or two weeks, the anger always subsides and life goes on business as usual. It wasn't always like this. Or was it? Can you think of a time when Black folks really did take the law into their own hands? Other than the Panthers I can't think of one. But I do know this; Black people are hesitant to call the police. This is because we have a long history of being on the receiving end of the night stick, billy club, baton, and trigger. When anyone in the community gets shot fifty times you'd think there'd be a more effective means for getting justice than candlelight vigils and marches. But sometimes bad things have to happen for us to show unity. At some point however there must be some accountability for the perpetrators. And not just a slap on the wrist as is usually the case. We all know that the boys in blue have not always been our friend. Do a poll in the "hood" and you'll find that the "Po-Po's" have more of a reputation for breaking the law themselves than protecting and serving the community. Incident after tragic incident only adds to the distrust Black folks have for law enforcement. The only explanation is that a Black man's (woman's) life seems to be of less value than a member of the police force which makes us very uncomfortable when it comes time to dial 911. In the Black community the fact of the matter is that people are afraid of the police just as much (if not more) than the criminals. And we're frustrated because we see neither justice nor any means of "get back" when it comes to these senseless crimes. So we end up wondering who to call when the *police* are breaking the law.

"Do you know why I pulled you over sir?"

"Er, uhm … is it because I'm Black?"

Hmm … You'd be amazed how easily even you could fit the description based on where you are, what time it is, what you're driving/riding in, and yes, the grade of your shade. Furthermore American society is not very forgiving of those who have been convicted (rightly or wrongly) and incarcerated. Never mind all the hot air about prison as a form of rehabilitation. But what really happens after "Tyrone" has paid his debt to society and reenters the general population faced with even more obstacles than the ones which landed him in the penile … sorry penal system in the first place? The cold, hard truth is that not many employers are exactly chomping at the bit to extend an opportunity to a convicted felon, or even a small time crook for that matter. And so most inmates who are released from jail and return to the same streets usually get caught up in the exact same activity and end right back up in the "pokey." What would have happened if there was no videotape of the Rodney King beating of the 90's? I'll tell you what, precisely the same thing that *did* happen. No conviction for the perpetrators. So the more things change the more they stay the same. My civil rights are different than my mother's civil rights. My child's civil rights are different than my civil rights. But unfortunately we still catch the same hell whenever we find ourselves tangled up in the criminal "justice" system. See, people play games with the truth every day. Just look at the jury system in this country.

Six to twelve individuals locked in a room sometimes for days until they come to a unanimous decision as to the fate of another human being. These jurors are selected based on such factors as age, sex, race, and background and the way they answer particular questions. For instance; "Is there any circumstance that would bias you towards this case?" For the "defendant's" sake I hope not. But people lie every day. Our judicial system is based upon the premise that anyone suspected of a crime is "innocent till proven guilty." But if you happen to be Black and your name ain't Orenthal chances are you'll be found guilty before you even have a chance to try on the bloody glove.

Have you noticed the increase in the number of police/crime scene investigation/courtroom drama shows on television these days? Seems like every other one is centered around some twisted, "cross dressing" doctor caught up in a diabolical plot to arrange his wife's murder gone bad." In fact, prime time television over the past few years has aired more of these whodunit murder mystery shows and crime dramas than ever before. What is this infatuation with the criminal justice system all about? I can't lie, I sometimes even find myself tuning into the reruns! And I know I'm not the only one. I don't know if there is a part of me that is subconsciously rooting for the "bad guys" or I'm just tuning in to see where the perpetrator shot himself in the foot. Either way I'm hooked. But the reality in most urban areas for Black folks is far from an episode of *"Brutal Justice."*

"You have the right to keep your mouth shut."

And so it goes. By the way, have you ever had a gun pulled on you? I have. And trust me it's not a good feeling baby. Especially from someone who in many instances looks like you in every way except for the badge pinned to his chest. Fortunately I'm still here to write about it. But I always wondered; Why do so many Black cops seem to have even more racist tendencies than their white partners? Probably the same reason so many Blacks go to white lawyers. The dreaded

F.O.A.B.P! No one in their right mind wants to face the prospect of spending even a night behind bars much less any type of bid that's for sure. That's because we all understand that jail is not normal. But it is one of the only effective ways to neutralize the Amerfrican and prevent him from reproducing. Once you've got him behind those gates he's basically extinct. Just another number. It's kinda like the homeless situation. One minute you see him, the next he's gone. Just like that. Out of sight and out of mind. There are literally thousands upon thousands of Blacks (and Hispanics) that can describe in chilling detail the horrors of prison life and its effects on the human mind and spirit. There are millions more who will never be able to. In America the Supreme Court are the gods when it comes to setting the standards and upholding the rulings and judgments that stand literally for generations. When it comes to the criminal justice system and your particular relationship to it however only you hold the key to your freedom and it is therefore up to you to protect it all costs.

Bottom Line: In the earliest African communal societies there was not even a word for jail since no one had ever gone to one. There was universal law. There are two types of crime out here; 1) crime against humanity and 2) crime against nature. But perhaps the biggest crime that is rarely acknowledged is the crime against SELF. Each day we lie, cheat and steal our way out of what is rightfully ours for no apparent reason whatsoever. There are seventeen and eighteen year old brothers and sisters locked up for life for a momentary lapse of judgment. Consequently a whole generation of potential leaders are lost or remain on pins and needles trying to avoid that third strike. Everybody knows Black (and Brown) males are going to jail at a far greater rate than any other group out here today. Whether it's for drug offenses, "wrong place wrong time" situations, domestic violence or crimes they didn't commit. It's time for us take stock of this and give the youth more alternatives than the dead end allure of fast cars and "easy" money. But the real bottom line has never changed. If you do the crime, just make sure you're prepared to do the time. Feel me?

13

POINTING FINGERS

MAMA: *Baby, I want you to change the world when you grow up okay?*

DAUGHTER: *(5yrs. old) I will Mommy.*

MAMA: *Promise me sweetie.*

DAUGHTER: *I promise Mommy!*

(Twenty years later) …

DAUGHTER: *But Mama, I just wanna do something to make a difference, y' know change the world!*

MAMA: *Honey it's time for you to grow up now. You can't change the world. You can only change yourself …*

This is the diet for today's youth. Mixed messages, lack of proper guidance and direction. Children do as you *do*, not as you say. They see the things we have forgotten how to. But what role do they play in the grand scheme of things? More importantly, what active role do you play in their growth and development? Since children are such unique and flexible creatures it is essential that they are given the proper nutrients from the time they enter the womb to the time they enter the world. Whenever I lost or misplaced my house keys my mother would say; "This is the last time I open this door for you." "Next time you lose your keys you don't come in." Period. And guess what, I never lost my keys after that. Well maybe once or twice but you get the point. Basic discipline and conduct are as important to a child's development as A's, B's, and SAT's. But too many times the emphasis is placed on the child's progress and advancement from grade to grade, from high school to college and so forth. This is the illusion. The only true advancement is from boyhood to manhood/ girlhood to womanhood. It took me a long time to come to grips with the reality that parents are just people with children. It is easy to scold a child for displaying bad manners until you listen to his father's. Just as it is natural to blame the child for her unruly behavior until you observe her Mama's. Seems like the priorities in the home have changed over the years as well. These days the streets, worldwide web, and peer pressure are raising our kids while the parents are either out of touch or out to lunch. Would you believe there are actually parents who have no problem whatsoever dishing out six figures to throw their daughter a "Sweet Sixteen" birthday bash? It's true. A young girl to her friend; "You're a virgin?" "I didn't know they had those anymore ..." And before too long you've got another unwed mother forced to grow up before she should have to. Babies continue to make babies, yet lack the skills to raise them. The youth of today need stronger role models now than ever before considering the pitfalls that lay so perilously in their path. And what do you expect? A twelve year old boy is just learning to pee straight and has no clue as to what to do when erections become a daily part of his routine. By this time it is almost too late to sit him down and talk about the "birds and the bees." On top of that parents are simply afraid. You would be surprised to know the amount of vital information that is withheld from the children out of the parents' fear, insecurity or just plain shame of their own personal conduct or past indiscretions. Some children don't even find out who their biological parent is till they reach adulthood! How does that kid grow up to be alright?

So we tell our kids to look both ways before crossing the street. But what happens when the crossing guards are fondling them? What happens is the parents usually never find out because the youth are too scared to say anything. I personally know several women who have told me they were touched inappropriately when they were small. But when I ask what their parents did when they found out they either say they were called liars or chastised for making up stories. A word to parents: L-I-S-T-E-N to your children!!! Stop talking so much and just listen. It's as simple as that. Later on you'll be glad you did. See, today's problems are the same as when you were coming up, only the circumstances have changed. Children are two hundred times more exposed here in the twenty-first century than they were in 1957 so you have to approach the conversation differently, but the issues remain the same. Eight and nine year olds are "doin' it on the bus" these days. And Mama is sittin' back in denial talkin' 'bout "Not *my* baby!" Yes YOUR BABY!! You gotta look deeper to get to what's really goin' on. Today's kids are more intelligent than ever which means they require more structure to help channel all of their creative energy.

On top of that, kids are always trying be like their parents. But this can be quite complicated because sometimes it's better for a child not to repeat some of the same behaviors that were passed down from Mommy or Daddy. Your Mama is your first image of God. This is true. Your father on the other hand is your first image of the world, and in the case of Black boys the first image of themselves. The Black father is potentially the most valuable asset to the community we have. Unfortunately he is also the most marked man in existence. And tragically, he is often absent from the crucial stages of his child's life for whatever reason. As the traditional two parent household has morphed into a new breed of parenting characterized by shared custody, supervised/unsupervised visits and society's newfound acceptance of same sex unions, the face of fatherhood is ever changing. A large percentage of marriages these days end in divorce, and guess who gets caught in the crossfire? It's ALWAYS the children. It has been well documented that divorce causes serious emotional wounds that often take years to heal. But fathers get a raw deal sometimes. 'Specially Black ones. The pressure and responsibility of bringing a child into this world is awesome enough as it is and we should applaud positive and wholesome examples of fatherhood which are plentiful in our community. See, your father is your first role model, mentor, teacher etc ... but this relationship between father and son in particular is very complex, in part because the overwhelming majority of men are afraid of INTIMACY. It's true. Teaching a boy how to be a man is more than teaching him how to change the oil or fix a leaky faucet (although that's part of it too). A lot of fathers underestimate the importance of just being around. It's the little things that children remember later on in life. Things like reading the Front page of the newspaper before checking out the Sports page. And what defines being a man anyway? Holding down a job? Being "responsible?" Paying bills on time? Possibly. But in essence, being a man starts simply by being around MEN. And usually, through this a boy can see how men carry themselves. What's the flip side? Another young male with too much time and testosterone on his hands. And the consequences of this? Just turn on your nightly news. It's no mystery why many of our children come home with D's, E's, and F's on their report cards. The mystery is how the parents (and grandparents) lost touch with their own flesh and blood in the first place. Television, video games and the Internet aside, it always comes back to Mommy and Daddy. Believe that.

Still, a funny thing happens within the circle of life. As a child grows from adolescence to adulthood the spotlight is shone upon him and the choices he makes (or doesn't make). But as she becomes "grown," hopefully stable and well adjusted, the focus of the camera lens is turned squarely on her PARENTS who will either be applauded for doing such a good job or looked at with raised eyebrows for not being around. You can usually tell how a child has been raised within minutes of observing his behavior. And the truth is, parents unwittingly pass on any number of complexes to their "pride and joy" simply because they have failed to address them in their own personal lives. This is why now more than ever we need useful elders to break the cycle. Give a child a new bicycle and he'll learn how to ride within a week. Give a child life lessons and she'll pass them on for the rest of her life. What more can you ask for?

THE CRYING GAME

Children are an investment in time, energy, and money. What happens all too often in cases of separation or divorce is the pitting of one parent against the other in order to feed the damaged ego of either parent. And what complicates the issue even further is the fact that most people (including parents) are not honest. True honesty is too painful for most. We act honest, but lie at the first opportunity to avoid the pain. This is very unhealthy for all parties involved. Money is usually the main culprit for marital strife, even though the fact is that most couples don't make enough individually to get divorced in the first place. On top of that, the child already has her favorite, and all you are doing is fostering distrust and confusion in whom you claim to be your "whole world." Psychologists have long researched and recognized the inherent emotional attachment between the child and his same sex parent. The term "Daddy's little girl" does ring true, but only in intervals. The constant link has and will always be between mother and daughter, father and son. And just as every mother has what it takes to make her daughter feel beautiful (unique, special), every father is equipped with the tools to guide his son in the right way. But only by EXAMPLE! Anyway, back to the investment. Anyone in their right mind who invests money, time, or energy into anything expects some sort of return on their investment. But why? Anyone truly IN TUNE with children is already wealthy. It's been proven time and again that regardless of background or circumstance any child can excel and contribute to society. Just as it has been proven that anyone can be a parent, from "Coach" at the Rec Center to Big Brother/Big Sister mentor to "stepmom/stepdad." Whether biological or surrogate, the key element to developing and sustaining any healthy relationship is TIME. Spending quality and meaningful time lets the child know she is more than just a pain in the you know what.

All parents have high hopes for their kids. It's just that sometimes they fail to examine the "conditions" they pass down to them. Then they wonder why Little Nique Nique is always fighting at school. Sometimes personalities just clash. For whatever reason we are drawn to certain people and repulsed by others. This dynamic applies to all relationships, friends and family alike. We naturally spend more time around those we feel comfortable with and less time around those we butt heads. But for some reason we tend to overlook this important dynamic when it comes to parent/child relationships. Just because they are "Mommy and Daddy" doesn't mean that their personalities will automatically blend with their children's. But it is still up to the parent to teach the life skills necessary for the child to grow and flourish in today's ever changing society. As a youth I was always encouraged to "speak proper English." (apparently what I had been speaking all along was broken). And since I never actually received any lessons on what exactly proper English was I became more and more confused as I grew and matured. Looking back, I realize that perhaps my parents believed that speaking this so called "proper English" would somehow take me farther in life and this was just their way of trying to make it easier for me to function in society. But now I realize that "Just be yourself" may have been more useful advice. But hey, at least they were there …

These days many of our youth are not so lucky. More Black babies are being born with blue eyes than ever before. And no I'm not talkin' about jungle fever folks. I'm referring to the "educational" system our children have been subjected to since the early days of civil rights, busing and integration. When you sent your child off to school this morning you assumed her teachers would provide her with the proper lessons and instruction to carry her to the next phase of life (or at least the next grade). A child's school plays a crucial role in her rise to greatness. Yet even today in this new millennium the standards and school curriculum are not reflective of the cultural diversity of its students. One of the most important (and intense) decisions a parent must make is whether to send his/her child to public, private, or "alternative" schools. This choice has all sorts of financial, religious, geographic and social implications. There is always the fear of kids slipping through the cracks and falling short of their full potential. And one need only take a look at the high school graduation rate in so many of our major cities to realize that it ain't all good in the 'hood. By now we all know there are more Black males in jail than in college today. So with all these challenges and much more facing our youth the last things they should have to worry about are out of date textbooks and overcrowded classrooms. By the way, do you know who exactly chooses your child's textbooks? Do you even CARE? Hmm ... On top of that kids seem to be much angrier these days. You hear it from teachers, coaches and guidance counselors alike; "Half the time they don't even show up for class!" I wonder why? Maybe it's because they feel there is more to learn on the streets than in the classroom where the curriculum is often outdated and/or culturally biased. Or perhaps they're just frustrated. Just like Mommy and Daddy.

Bottom Line: Children are a direct reflection of their parents. There are no two ways around it. You're good with kids right? Wonderful. Now it's time to be good *to* them. Let them know where they come from, the greatness they possess and where that comes from as well. Hopefully this will be enough to make them see the world and where they fit into it differently than everywhere else they get their information. And another thing; children have no idea they're not good enough until you tell them. That's right YOU! Hell, they don't even know what being good enough *means* till you teach them! Your job is to help them become who they came here to be, not to weigh them down with your issues. Fortunately they chose you for this position. So don't just praise them when they do well and scold them when they do wrong. It's about being visible examples as to what right and wrong actually is. 'Cause at the end of the day whether we choose to admit it or not we need them just as much (if not more) than they need us. Most importantly, show your kids love and let them know they are perfectly fine just the way they are. They'll appreciate you for it later. And who knows, maybe then all of our children will grow up to be valedictorians.

14

THE GOOD NEWS

When you believe in yourself, strange things start to happen. People, places, and things begin to appear differently than they did before as do the self-imposed chains you've been wearing all this time. Soon others begin to take note as well. Ali had his opponent beat before he even threw the first punch. How was this possible? It was his confidence that instilled fear in the hearts of those that dared step into the ring with him. Imagine the audacity of predicting the exact round you're going to knock out your opponent then going out and doing it! But also imagine if Ali had gone to war instead of standing up for what he believed in. There's no doubt he'd have been looked at quite differently than he is today. You see brothers and sisters, sometimes the only voice you can trust is your own, especially when times get rough. And if you listen closely to that voice you really and truly can make a DIFFERENCE.

So other day I found myself in my local public library just checkin' out some books when I happened to notice a photo exhibit in one of the large conference rooms. There were probably ten or so blown-up Black and white photographs hanging from the walls as I walked past. Something told me to turn around and check it out so I stepped inside to catch a closer look. A small brochure identified the exhibit as RECONSTRUCTING: 1870-1930, A Photo Essay. Apparently the collection was shot and compiled by a local photojournalist and author. After briefly reading his bio, my eyes ran up to the bland white walls of the otherwise empty room. Gazing at the images before me was like stepping into a time machine, one that I had never seen, heard or read about in his-story class. Each photograph was more riveting than the last, illustrating the African experience in the Americas, the Caribbean and the continent itself. The first one appeared to be taken around the turn of the twentieth century. It showed a group of Black teenage boys, dressed in jackets, ties, knickers and hard shoes. They carried tattered, dusty looking books and appeared to be coming from school. Simple enough scene, think it was Harlem, but even more fascinating were the expressions on the young men's faces. They looked genuinely happy. They were neat, well groomed, and stood tall with their backs completely straight. No slouching, slumping or posing. Now I know clothes and class are two different things, but the young men in that photo really did look sharp, intelligent and alive, quite different than what you routinely see today. The next photograph showed a large group of young people, probably in their twenties, apparently outside a Black Church in the South in the early 1900's. The ladies sported their lovely hats, (tilted of course) respectable dresses, and welcoming smiles. They seemed so regal and dignified; the men so determined and distinguished looking. Oh, and FEARLESS, like they really had PLANS. And it all came bursting through the frame. And there were more. Image after image captured a distinct emotion and conjured up a spirit inside of me that made me really think. "Damn, they look so PROUD!" From the pictures on the wall you would never, ever suspect that these royal looking Black people had just been "set free" from years and years of dehumanizing treatment and forced labor. Their smiles were genuine, even the gaze and weathered faces of the elders were unflinching, and the delicate beauty of the women mesmerizing. Staring at these images made me ask myself "WHERE HAVE THESE PEOPLE GONE???" And if they are no longer with us, where are their offspring? It was then that I experienced an incredible moment of clarity that hit me squarely in the chest, nearly taking my breath away. And the first thing that came to me was; "They haven't gone anywhere.

WE'RE STILL HERE!!!

So that's what I look for these days when I walk down the street. And every time I see that same glint in my brother/sister's eye I know that everything is gonna be alright. See my friends, there is light at the end of the tunnel. And when it's all said and done the fear of a Black penis can be a catalyst for real change, both individually as well as collectively. It can spur growth, development, self-determination and most of all ACCOUNTABILITY. You see my beloved brothers and sisters, we can no longer continue to urinate on the contributions and sacrifices of those who came before us. For in our ancient African incarnations we would pour out libations to celebrate the great lives and accomplishments of our ancestors. Today we "pour out a 'lil liquor" for our dead homies ... So although times have changed and we are now faced with unique challenges and circumstances, the fact remains that we are still here. And at the end of the day we will continue to be the torch-bearers for creativity, ingenuity, and originality. It is who we are. Still you ask; "But what can I do to make a difference?" "And just how can I give back to my community?" Well brotha, here are three ways you can start:

1) **BE YOURSELF!** And I do mean yourself, not somebody you feel you have to be based on your upbringing, environment, or pressure from family or friends. Dig deep, get to know and appreciate all the unique attributes you bring to the table and strive to be the greatest YOU that ever walked the face of the Earth!

2) **ARTICULATE YOUR VISION!!** This step takes courage my beloved. But you will see in the long run that anything worthwhile takes both courage and sacrifice. That's the whole point. Do not be afraid to let others in on your plans, hopes and dreams. You'd be surprised how many people will be willing to help you along your way.

And once you do manifest your heart's truest desire you will be amazed by how valuable an asset you have become to your community.

3) MAKE 'EM CALL YOUR NAME!!! Once you've taken the first two steps they will have no other choice. But in order to make them call your name it is essential that you finish what you start. I repeat; you must FINISH WHAT YOU START! Then not even the sky will be the limit trust me. No, trust YOU! And finally my brilliant, beautiful, intelligent, proud, dignified, captivating, regal, relentless, elegant, exquisite, and fearless brother/sister, once you've completed these steps there is only one thing that is left for you to do.

SHOW SOMEBODY ELSE!!!

ACKNOWLEDGEMENTS

To all of you who have nurtured, inspired and encouraged me in life. I deeply appreciate your patience, love, and kindness. You know who you are.

NOTES

1. **ix** excerpt from Voices in the Mirror (An Autobiography) by Gordon Parks pg. 342; Published by DOUBLEDAY Copyright 1990 by *Gordon Parks.*

2. Chapter 1: **pg. 9** "black;" MERRIAM WEBSTER ONLINE Copyright 2005 by Merriam Webster Incorporated.

3. Chapter 3 **:pg. 33** excerpt from Playing In The Dark, Whiteness and the Literary Imagination by Toni Morrison; Harvard University Press, Cambridge, Mass., 1992 Copyright 1992.

4. Chapter 4: **pg. 42** excerpt from article "An American Journey;" Tuesday, Oct. 18, The Guardian by Oona King; source; Dalton Conley.

5. Chapter 9: **pg. 95** "Pornography;" Microsoft Encarta Online Encyclopedia 2007 http://encarta.msn..com 1997-2007Microsoft Corporation.

6. **pg. 98** excerpt from "Coming Apart," pg. 42 from You Can't Keep a Good Woman Down by Alice Walker, Harvest 1981.

Index

978-0-595-44857-9
0-595-44857-7